MY YEAR IN A
Yurt

God's Hope & Healing in a
Tiny House Lifestyle!

Jen McGeehan

ISBN 978-1-64140-557-7 (paperback)
ISBN 978-1-64140-559-1 (hardcover)
ISBN 978-1-64140-558-4 (digital)

Copyright © 2018 by Jen McGeehan

All rights reserved. No part of this publication may be reproduced, distributed, or transmitted in any form or by any means, including photocopying, recording, or other electronic or mechanical methods without the prior written permission of the publisher. For permission requests, solicit the publisher via the address below.

Christian Faith Publishing, Inc.
832 Park Avenue
Meadville, PA 16335
www.christianfaithpublishing.com

Printed in the United States of America

Dedication

As children, teenagers, even young adults, we are seldom able to recognize the many ways we mirror our parents. I was thirty-eight years old, a wife, and a mother of a young daughter and son before I acknowledged that my entrepreneurial skills were a birth gift from my mother. By that time, she had enjoyed her heavenly residence for sixteen years, having succumbed to lung cancer at the age of forty-four. To this day, I am grateful for her teaching in the areas of baking and sewing, the importance of list making, and her steely temperament that never gave up. She was a savvy business owner before it became popular for women to *bring home the bacon*. Her tiny company, Wild Designs by Gretchen, provided employment for a half-dozen women, decorating with bright tissue paper flowers a variety of retail establishments including Neimen Marcus. Way to go, Mom!

Well into my fifties, I realized my writing skills were a birth gift from my father. Although he never pursued a literary career, his pen and paper musings demanded preservation. And the story he wrote, detailing the bullet wounds he suffered while serving our country during WWII, wrapped around his sustaining faith in God, became the central theme of his memorial service on August 18, 2012. Dad loved words. *Toiling, ebullient,* and *umbrage* were just a few of his favorites. Don't ask me how he came up with *Puce* as my nickname.

How grateful I am for the opportunity to dedicate this book to my precious earthly parents. Thank you, Mom and Dad, for your inexhaustible love and support, for seeing and encouraging talents in me that I could not see in myself, for sacrificing, and for following God's call as my parents. The birth gifts you passed on to me have carried me through the joys and the trials of life, gifts that will shine the light on the everlasting love and faithfulness of our heavenly Father through His Son, Jesus Christ, and the Holy Spirit—God's greatest gifts to mankind!

In loving memory of:

Gretchen Gerrish Clay
November 4, 1936~December 6, 1980

William Gordon Clay
April 26, 1925~August 9, 2012

Special Dedication

Although I never met her in person, I had a number of phone conversations with Becky Kemery, author of the highly acclaimed *Yurts: Living in the Round*. She was very encouraging as I shared my vision for *My Year in a Yurt* and had even agreed to provide an endorsement. Our final conversation was brief—her voice was weak and I could hear a steady hiss-hiss in the background. Just prior to ending our chat, I took a chance. "Becky, are you ill?"

She responded with a faint, "Yes."

"Is it life-threatening?"

"Yes." With that, I promised to pray for her and call her in a month. "Thank you" were her final words to me. Months later, I did a Google search after she failed to respond to my phone calls and e-mails. I was shocked to discover that she had succumbed to cancer! I was also surprised to find out just how much we had in common. We were born just seventeen days apart in April 1956. She passed away the day of my father's memorial service—August 18, 2012. We both held a deep appreciation for nature, and we loved the written word.

Becky, you are greatly missed by your family, your friends, and those who were just getting to know you!

Becky Kemery
April 25, 1956~August 18, 2012

Acknowledgments

The written word cannot adequately express my sincere gratitude to the scores of family members and friends who have encouraged me to share my thoughts and experiences through *My Year in a Yurt*. I believe it really began when dear friend, Belinda, decided we should start an American Christian Writer's (ACW) chapter in Big Bear, California. The bug-to-write beyond the typical work-related newsletters, advertising campaigns, and press releases was further flamed when I attended an ACW Conference. And from there, the ball began to roll!

A special thank you goes out to Amy, Sherri, and Catherine. Through your individual prayer requests, the Lord used the three of you in a most miraculous way—to write words of faith, hope, love, perseverance, healing, and restoration! I give my heartfelt thanks to Bob and Lois Daniels, the best example of surrogate parents on the planet. Bob, thank you for reading every word I have written, for your volumes of encouragement, and for painstakingly noting those nasty typos no writer ever wants to see in their manuscript. Lo, I am so grateful that you were faithful in sharing God's love for me, for your patience as He quietly wooed me unto Him, for every time you invited me to church even though I always said no, and for the precious Bible you gave to me so many years ago! Meeting you and then having the privilege of working together at La Habra Fashion Square were His divine appointments. God heard every whispered prayer over the course of the next thirty-four years, and I will eternally thank Him for sending you. I love you both!

Thank you, Darlene, for your meticulous attention to every detail of the "Yurt Resource Guide." You treated this *special assignment* as if it were your own baby. Thank you, Pat, for always believing in me, for encouraging me, and for never complaining when you woke up in the middle of the night only to discover that I was sitting at my computer with the lantern on, wildly hitting the keyboard to get a few more thoughts out of my head and onto the screen. Your playful and witty words are woven throughout this book, adding a touch of spice and creative flair I could never have provided. I love you eternally!

I thank Christian Faith Publishing and Marie Lewis for believing that this story of God's healing and restoration should continue through the publication of the 2nd Edition of *My Year in a Yurt*! Thank you for believing in me.

This opportunity and experience brings my entire life full circle. Thank you for believing in me! And to my Lord and Savior, Jesus Christ. It is only through the indwelling of Your Holy Spirit that I move and breathe. Your Word has been "a lamp unto my feet and a light unto my path." You opened the door for me. You held my hand, and we walked through together. May "Your will be done on earth as it is in heaven." I praise You, and I thank You!

{
Now to Him who is able to do exceedingly abundantly beyond all that we ask or think, according to the power that works within us, to Him be the glory in the church and in Christ Jesus to all generations forever and ever. Amen.

Ephesians 3:20–21
}

THE YURT PROJECT...
WE'RE ON THE MOVE!

Image Courtesy of Yurts of Hawaii

The Tiny House Movement has arrived in Hawaii, specifically the Big Island! The Yurt Project, birthed through the publication of *My Year in a Yurt!*, is a partnership with Yurts of Hawaii and is dedicated to providing a move-in-ready yurt to a very special individual, couple, or family annually. Partner with us as we make a difference…one yurt at a time!

Ten percent of net proceeds from the purchase of *My Year in a Yurt!* is donated to The Yurt Project. Additional financial and/or materials donations can be made, with a tax-deductible receipt provided, by going to www.theyurtproject.com/yurtproject.

808.985.9715
www.yurtsofhawaii.com
yurtshawaii@gmail.com

"In recent years, the growth of the Big Island has spurred a crucial need for practical alternatives to expensive housing. In today's economy, these issues are felt even more crucially by all of us. A time for creative solutions is at hand. It isn't time to reinvent the wheel; it is time to rediscover it! We work hand-in-hand with our clients to design a yurt best-suited to their individual needs and budget." Melissa Fletcher, Owner

Map Of Big Island
of Hawaii

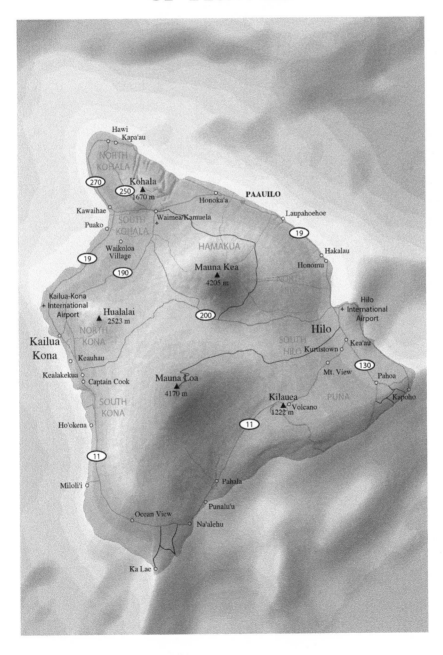

Our "Love Yurt!"

Contents

Preface

In September 2011, my hubby, Pat, and I stuffed our most cherished and needed belongings into a forty-foot Matson container, shipped our Chevy truck and Mini Cooper, flew one horse and goat air cargo, then, with bulging roll-on luggage, moved to the Big Island of Hawaii. Due to our devastating financial situation, we embraced the unique opportunity to rent our Hawaii realtor's twelve-acre property in the rural town of Paauilo, complete with a 450 not-so-square-foot yurt. "What the heck is a yurt?" you might ask…

Ours was a twenty-four-foot diameter, Mongolian-inspired tent, constructed of vinyl siding and roof, with a huge acrylic skylight dome and lattice interior walls. It offered a nice kitchenette and small potbelly stove. The bathroom, located under the backside of the attached lanai, required a quick jaunt down a lava rock pathway. Like many residents of Hawaii, we lived off-grid, which meant we had no city-provided utilities. Instead, rain water was captured in enormous twelve- and eighteen-thousand-gallon tanks, electricity was a gift from the sun via solar panels perched on the roof of the lanai, gas was provided when we filled the twenty-gallon propane tank inconveniently located under the yurt, and TV, phone, and Internet were beamed down through two five-foot satellite dishes positioned under a huge Ohia tree in the immediate backyard! (When the second dish arrived, Pat began to refer to our little love yurt as the Starship Enterprise!)

The key to the huge paradigm shift of our lives came when God opened a door for us to move. We not only recognized it—we took it! Was our move to Hawaii, and a funky yurt, His new beginning for us? You bet! Just like millions of Americans across the country, we were adjusting to a "new normal." Our savings was nonexistent. Our home had not yet sold—after being on the market for three and a half years.

And we were carrying debt that totaled over $600,000! At the time of our exodus, we could see no light at the end of the dark, frightening tunnel. We knew it would take a God-sized miracle to pull us out of the financial pit we had found ourselves in.

My Year in a Yurt began as a prayer for three desperate girlfriends. It then turned into a blog on my Facebook page, offering support to women experiencing their own debilitating struggles while adjusting to their personal version of a "new normal." These women suffered from anxiety, stress, health issues, lack of sleep, fear, frustration, and confusion. A few ended up at the hospital or felt they were on their way to checking in! Truth be told, there is "One who sticks closer than a brother," who promises to take our burdens, who loves us unconditionally, who is there to guide and direct us every step of the way. His name is Jesus Christ. With Him, "all things are possible."

Living in a yurt, off-grid, away from family and close friends had its challenges. There were times of frustration and loneliness, times when I couldn't help but question God and His plan for Pat and me. But through this faith-stretching process, God has taught me valuable life lessons, blessing us exponentially as we humbled ourselves and walked the path He stretched out before us. These are the lessons and the blessings I believe He wants me to share with you! Wherever you are, whatever your situation, He is always there to guide, protect, and provide. Learning to trust Him, to lean on Him, to follow Him is the answer.

I look forward to hearing how He blesses you in your own journey through *My Year in a Yurt*.

The Exodus

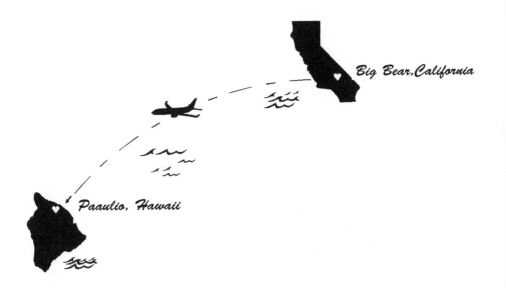

Big Bear, California

Paauilo, Hawaii

September 2011

Say "Yes" to a Yurt?

The dream of living in Hawaii was planted deep within our hearts years prior to actually making the move-of-faith, as I like to call it. In 2002, Pat and I took our first Big Island vacation after less than a full year of marriage. His high school buddy, Dick, had moved his wife and young family to a six-acre coffee farm ten years earlier. As we spent seven glorious days enjoying the aloha spirit, we too began to embrace what this paradise had to offer.

Seven years later, and after two back surgeries for work-related injuries, Pat retired from a thirty-one-year career in the fire service. During this emotionally and physically stressful time, one additional stress landed squarely on our shoulders: sell the house!

It was the fall of 2008, and the reality of economic collapse had begun. We had just returned from our first reconnaissance trip to the Big Island, confident that it was time to pull up stakes and make the dream a reality. We both believed, with 100 percent certainty, that our custom-built dollhouse in Big Bear, California, would sell quickly...very quickly. But after three and a half years in a virtually nonexistent real estate market, our confidence level plummeted to a negative zero. Originally, our house was priced at $1,100,000. By the summer of 2011, it had dropped to $575,000 with no viable offers. We continued to have faith that God could sell it, even in a snowstorm, and that He would bring a buyer at just the right time. We just couldn't understand why He was taking so long. It's hard to describe living in a home that has been on the market for 1,265 days. In my three decades of buying and selling homes, the longest it took to close an escrow was four and a half months, and that felt like an eternity!

During those three and a half long years, we watched our equity dwindle from over $500,000 to zero as our debt, including an interest-only mortgage, consistently increased to well over $600,000. We were now living a financial nightmare, with absolutely no visible way out. By July of 2011, serious decisions had been made. We joined American Consumer Credit Counseling, consolidating our credit card debt into one somewhat manageable monthly payment. If we stayed on track, we would show a zero balance in four short years. Short? Not to me. All bank credit cards were cancelled, and we painstakingly began the adjustment from living on credit to living solely on our monthly income. I was so angry that we had gotten ourselves into this position that I was more than happy to finally live within our means, whatever that meant! It actually felt good to take charge of our finances, to say "no" to the lie that a person, couple, family can't survive without credit cards. We were out to prove them wrong. We not only would survive, but we would eventually, with God's help, thrive! How? We really had no idea except to follow the Bible's guidelines. No matter what, we would continue to tithe ten percent of our gross income.

Later that July, I received an e-mail from John and Karen, offering us the opportunity to travel to Hawaii to ranch-sit their twenty-acre paradise for the entire month of October. I had met John almost four years earlier through an Internet inquiry as I searched for a suitable place to board our horse and three goats when the time finally came to move. John had provided a plethora of island-living information. And we even rented their guest room during one of four reconnaissance trips. As I stared at the e-mail on my computer screen, I knew what our answer would be. Ashley, our oldest daughter, was getting married on October 22, and Chris, our only son, was entering the United States Coast Guard a day later. So I penned a painful response, "It just isn't possible." Thankfully, I sent a copy to Pat. The next morning changed our lives forever...

By mid-morning, Pat had enjoyed his customary cup of hot tea while catching up on e-mails sent the night prior. He found me in our bedroom, suggested we hop into our indoor Jacuzzi to "chat about John's offer." (I hadn't even had a chance to mention it to him.)

As the bubbles swirled around us, causing steam to cloud our view out the French windows and doors, a view to our future began to come into focus. "Pat, there is simply no way we can go. We've got the wedding on October 22, and I have to be there when Chris heads off to boot camp," I reasoned. He was very patient as I rattled off all the reasons we couldn't possible do this. And then, the door began to squeak open. "Jen, I think John's offer is a lily pad for us to move. We can stay at their place for three weeks, fly back for the wedding and boot camp send-off, then return to Hawaii permanently," he said, with a look of little boy expectancy all over his face! My jaw dropped as I tried to grasp hold of the suggestion he was making.

"But what about the house? It hasn't sold," I replied.

"Our realtor can continue to market it. We don't have to be here. When it sells, it sells."

"But where will we live after John and Karen return from their trip?"

"I have no idea. Let's just trust God with the details," he said in a matter-of-fact tone of voice. We sat in utter silence for many minutes, quietly digesting the possibilities set before us.

I then looked him straight in the eye and said, "I'm in! Let's go." Our Hawaiian journey began that miraculous morning! By noon, we had called John and Karen to accept their generous offer, announcing that we were, in fact, finally moving to Hawaii.

John said, "We've had that same effect on two other families. We will help you make the transition." Then, like a bullet out of a pistol, I started to look for a property to rent after October.

I hate to move. I really do. In addition to bi-annual visits to the dentist, renting a home is right up there on my "don't" list. In my entire fifty-five years of life, I have only rented twice. The first time was an apartment for five years directly after graduating from high school. The second time was a five-month stint while we were completing the building of our Big Bear home. In our current financial situation, renting was our *only option*. So I grasped this opportunity with all the gusto I could muster. I contacted rental companies on the Big Island, as well as searched the VRBO.com (Vacation Rental by Owner) listings. It quickly became obvious that finding a home with enough property to house our horse and three goats would be expensive and hard to come by. (I secretly wondered how on earth we would ever qualify.)

After a full week of research, I decided to call Bailey, our Hawaii realtor extraordinaire. I wanted to not only share our exciting move news but also see if he knew of any rentals we could consider. He couldn't believe that after three and a half years and four reconnaissance trips, we were finally making the oceanic jump. Bailey knows everyone in the Paauilo area, and although we hadn't yet purchased a home from him, he knew we eventually would. And by this time, we considered Bailey a good friend.

A few days later, I received an e-mail from him containing a most interesting offer...

"Why don't you rent our yurt? There's plenty of room for your animals, and it will give you a chance to experience life off-grid," he penned. As I once again stared at my computer screen, I thought back to reconnaissance trip number 3...

Bailey's Paauilo yurt property also includes a guest studio. It was this studio we stayed in while viewing a dozen or so potential properties. We absolutely loved his place, the lush grass-covered rolling hills, the stately Ohia trees dotting the land, the ocean in the distance. It was so peaceful, so quiet, so healing. And it was during this trip that Pat and I took a quick peek inside his empty yurt. Up to that point, I had never seen a yurt, inside or out. I didn't even know how to spell this word, as it had never once entered my vocabulary. "What the heck is a yurt?" I remember asking Bailey, as we talked on the phone one afternoon.

Thinking back to our stay on his unusual property allowed me the opportunity to do a quick mental review of his yurt: the acrylic-domed roof, the lattice interior walls, the quaint potbelly stove, light wood laminate flooring, and wrap-around lanai.

Very interesting. I concluded. Then, I quickly wrote back, "How much per month?"

His speedy response? "Eight hundred per month, and bring all the animals!"

I have to admit that although Pat was very excited to become yurt dwellers, I had serious concerns. *Live in one room? Twenty-four feet in diameter? Off-grid?* My questions had questions. Could I actually do this? And what would my friends and family say? After sharing my concerns with Pat, we both concluded that this was God's plan for us, that He had opened this door, a yurt door that would eventually lead to financial freedom…in a most unusual way. I called Bailey with our commitment to say yes to his yurt and twelve gorgeous acres, starting November 1. Unbelievable, but true!

Renting our realtor's yurt has truly been a blessing. We had just enough money for the first month's rent but not enough for the customary security deposit. Any other potential landlord would have insisted on a thorough credit check. Due to our devastating financial condition, we would never have passed as sound renters. But our relationship with Bailey, developed over a four-year period, created a situation whereby no security deposit or credit check was required. It was a marriage made in heaven!

Eighteen years ago, as a member of my church choir, I was deeply moved by a song we sang at an Easter musical. "God Will Make A Way," written and conducted by Don Moen, has forever stayed in my heart. In 1990, his sister's family lost their eldest son in a car accident as they were traveling between Texas and Colorado. He was unable to be with them in the aftermath, but in his grief for them, he found solace by writing the song's words while on a plane trip the following day. This divinely inspired song was his way of providing comfort for the survivors. During intense times of need, whether for myself or someone else, Don's words bubble to the surface of my consciousness, and I find encouragement to go on…

God will make a way, when there seems to be no way. He works in ways we cannot see. He will make a way for me. He will be my guide. Hold me closely to His side. With love and strength for each new day. He will make a way, He will make a way.

{
Jesus said to him, "I am the way, and the truth, and the life; no one comes to the Father, but through Me."

John 14:6
}

YURT FACTOID:

Yurt—A Tatar word for house, now in general use, replacing myriad tribal terms.

Put Him on a Plane? (Part 1)

Our cross-oceanic move from the pristine mountains of Southern California to the rich, rolling pastureland of the Hamakua Coast of Hawaii was anything but typical. Most people do not whittle down their earthly possessions to whatever fits inside a forty-foot shipping container, drop their keys off with their cars at a dock, nor, and here's the biggie, trailer their twenty-nine-year-old equine and two-year-old goat to the "cargo" area of an international airport! On September 14, 2011, this is exactly what we did. It's the story of how we flew Smoke, my Palomino Appaloosa, and Gerdie, our Nubian goat, to the Big Island that always causes an abrupt pause in the conversation. "You did what?" they ask, with disbelief in their shocked voices.

Let's back up four years. Initially, the suggestion of flying Smoke 2,500 miles over the Pacific Ocean was met with my "Absolutely *not*! We'll just have to wait until he dies!" matter-of-fact reply.

Pat casually responded, "Well, I'll miss you because I am going." I cried myself to sleep that night. I would miss him too! However, the next morning brought a modicum of hope.

"We'll find a way together" was the verbal salve Pat administered on my hurting heart. Over the course of the next few weeks, I made a number of inquiry phone calls.

"How exactly do you fly a horse to Hawaii?" was my repetitive question. Each shipper had a different mode of travel to the airport, but all insisted that it wasn't any harder than trailering a horse up a mountain road. "Really?"

"Yes, really." After hearing the process three times, I began to realize that it wasn't as scary as I had imagined. And in time, I accepted the fact that Smoke would eventually fly the friendly skies. My research led me to place my faith in Pacific Airlift. They seemed to have the best reputation in transporting everything from snakes to rhinos safely from point A to point B! Surely they could handle my beloved equine and goats. To help calm me down, Andee, the office manager, shared that a few years back, they flew a forty-two-year-old horse to Hawaii, and they still receive a Christmas card each December. Whew! That was a huge boost to my confidence level. After numerous phone calls over a three-year period, Andee announced, with a giggle, "You are our longest-standing nonflight customer." "Well, what do you expect when your house refuses to sell!" I jokingly responded.

Whether the house sold or not, we were moving in seven short weeks! What elation. I called Andee and booked Smoke's flight for Friday, September 16. When I asked about flying our three goats, she said, "No problem. We'll just add them in." It's quite exhausting to prepare a horse and three goats to fly, especially to Hawaii. The USDA (United States Department of Agriculture) provides the owner with an extensive list of medical requirements and timelines. Rabies is a huge deal, as is proper pet identification through a microchip or tattoo, a long list of vaccinations, and clearance of potential diseases. As you can imagine, there is no room for error. If something goes wrong, they simply ship your pets back to the mainland. OMG! That caused a few sleepless nights as I envisioned myself in Hawaii and Smoke on his way back to LAX cargo! No way! So I was extremely meticulous in my own personal timeline with the vet, as well as the contract from Pacific Airlift. Every *t* had to be crossed, and every *i* had to get its dot.

My vet came four different times, giving each animal its microchip injection, various anti-infectious shots, follow-up check, and the final parasite spray down accompanied by the all-important medical release paperwork. As an added precaution against leg injuries, I purchased special leg wraps for Smoke. Honestly, you would have thought he was Secretariat. Well, he is to me! In the midst of preparing the animals to fly, I had to finish my own preparations. This required four yard sales, distributing furniture, household goods, and clothing to family, friends, and local consignment shops, separating what was to go to my girlfriend's office for use upon my occasional return trips, from what would get stuffed into the shipping container, from what was to come with me on my flight, from what went to the dump, and on and on and on! My piles had piles! Then came the plan.

At 8:00 p.m. on Friday night, September 15, my wonderful neighbor, Mike, would pull up to our front yard with his four-horse trailer. We would load Smoke and the goats, along with their necessary hay and travel gear, plus my own personal luggage. We would drop the animals off at the Pacific Airlift LAX Cargo area, and Mike would drop me off at a local hotel for six important hours of sleep. At 6:00 a.m. the following morning, I would take a shuttle and catch my own early morning flight to Kailua-Kona. If all went as planned, I would arrive two hours in advance of the animals. Have you ever heard the saying, "Life is what happens when you're busy making plans?"

Two weeks prior to takeoff, we hit the first bump in the runway of our changing lives. During my dozen or so phone conversations with Andee, she led me to believe that the three goats would be an "add-on." Not much over the $3,000 it would cost to give Smoke his flight wings. That was good news. We had bought our oldest Nubian goat, Tinkerbelle, when she was four months old. Then five years later, we had her repeatedly violated over a five-week period, which produced twin girls—Sister Bertrille (Bertie) and Gertrude (Gerdie.) The girls were better than dogs, full-on members of our family. I gave Andee a call because I hadn't yet received the contract, confirming all vital travel information, including the total amount due! The fax machine soon whipped into gear, producing all the requested paperwork. And there it was—bomb number 1.

They were charging us an additional $3,000 to ship the goats! That would be a total of $6,000 for all the animals! I knew there was no way we could possibly afford $6,000 to get these beloved pets to Hawaii. The only way we could finance the move was by selling my custom-built MD Barn to a neighbor down the road. Other than that financial blessing, we were moving on a wing and a prayer! "Now what?" I whined to Pat. Finally, the painful decision was made to leave the three goats behind. I can't describe the sadness in my heart. I had been present at their birth, taking over the responsibility of milking, straining, and then bottle-feeding Bertie and Gerdie when Tinkerbelle decided to get even with us for her "repeated violations." Oh brother! I loved those goats, but we just didn't have an extra $3,000 sitting around waiting to be spent. Now I had a new challenge—to find one home for three goats, and within fourteen days! I prayed about this. I prayed about this a lot!

{
Are not five sparrows sold for two cents? And yet not one of them is forgotten before God.

Luke 12:6
}

YURT FACTOID:

Yurts are one of the oldest indigenous forms of architecture, carrying the energy of tribal nomads crossing Asian steppes from millennia past.

Put Him on a Plane (Part 2)

During the fourth of our four "moving sales," our friends, the Geigers, stopped by. We filled them in on our upcoming move, and then a miracle occurred. I casually mentioned that we couldn't take the goats and that we were looking for the right home for them. They literally jumped in with, "Maybe we'll take them!" I couldn't believe it. After mentioning it to dozens of people, had God brought the perfect solution? All things are possible. As excited as I was at that moment, I was also feeling the pain of losing them. The Geigers said they would think about it and call us in a few days. Two nights later, as Pat and I finished a delicious dinner at the Sweet Basil Bistro in town, I started to cry. With his gentle hand on my arm, he asked me what was up. "I already miss the girls. I don't want to leave them." In my mind, I could see their trusting brown eyes gazing up at me, while feeling the soft warmth of their coats as I snuggled each one.

Pat, in his kind way, reminded me that we just didn't have the money to fly them to Hawaii. Then, his eyes widened, and he said, "Why don't we take just one? Yes, that's what we'll do! Surely we can afford just one, right?" I quickly agreed, mopping up my tear-stained cheeks. Hope was restored in the blink of a teardrop. The next morning, as I was flipping pancakes, the Geigers showed up unannounced at our front door. We welcomed them in, poured each a cup of steaming coffee, and then we told them we had an announcement. Their happy faces drooped just a bit as Mr. Geiger said, "You've decided to take the girls." We saw their disappointment, so we quickly told them of our decision to take just Gerdie. Their smiles immediately returned as they shared the fact that they really had only wanted two goats, but they had finally agreed to take all three since they were a little family. So the decision was made—Gerdie would get her own wings right alongside Smoke! We all enjoyed the next hour together, consuming our pancakes while making plans for the "great goat exchange." Wow! God did another miracle!

At noon on Wednesday, September 14, just two days before we were set to fly, I faxed the final vet check and release paperwork, as well as authorization to auto-transfer the $3,800 ($3,000 for Smoke and $800 for Girdie). An hour later, while making a final furniture drop-off at a local antique store, I called Andee just to confirm that all was in order. Then, bomb number 2 dropped. Andee confirmed that she had received all necessary paperwork and the auto-transfer of funds. "We'll see you tonight!" was her closing remark.

"What?" (I was positive I had heard her wrong.)

"We'll see you tonight at LAX" was her matter-of-fact reply.

I reminded her that we were doing the drop-off tomorrow night, leaving very early the following morning.

She said, "No. You go tonight."

"No, we don't. We fly Friday morning," I said loudly into the phone. I quickly pulled the car to the side of the road and wildly searched for the paperwork. There it was, as clear as the azure Hawaiian waters. We were flying the early morning of the sixteenth, not the fifteenth as she had insisted.

She stuttered and then said, "I don't know what happened, but you have to be there tonight at 11:00 p.m.!"

"Are you kidding me?" I practically screamed into the phone. Not only was I flying my animals, I was leaving California permanently! Everything had to go. I wasn't coming back to my house, ever! How could I possibly be ready to go in six short hours? (Cargo flights for animals are only scheduled once per month. So if we missed this flight, the animals would have to stay in California for another month. This simply could *not* happen!) The next six hours felt like I was in the eye of a tornado! As I was driving home, I called Pat to put him on red alert. We were leaving twenty-four hours earlier than scheduled! He was as calm as a cucumber, asking what he needed to do to help. I don't remember my response. Then, I called my neighbor to see if he could take us to LAX that night instead of the following evening. I had to change my flight to Hawaii, change my hotel reservation, and call our friends in Hawaii to verify that they could pick us up, with trailer in tow, a full twenty-four hours earlier than planned. Miraculously, everyone was able to accommodate my little emergency. Boy, was I relieved!

When I arrived home, I flew into first gear, literally zooming from room to room, grabbing last-minute items and cramming them into my already full suitcases. Items I had intended to pack and mail to Hawaii were pitched into a fifty-gallon water container. The container, along with two additional boxes, had to come along with the animals, whether Andee liked it or not. (She owed me, I reasoned.) Time was so tight that I never had a chance to say good-bye to our other two goats; Chloe, our kitty; or my beloved home. In retrospect, that was probably God's way of making my exodus less emotional, but certainly not less stressful!

> When you pass through the waters, I will be with you; and through the rivers, they will not overflow you. When you walk through the fire, you will not be scorched; nor will the flame burn you. For I am the Lord your God, the Holy One of Israel, your Savior.
>
> Isaiah 43:2–3a

YURT FACTOID:

For 150 years, during the thirteenth and fourteenth centuries, the yurt-dwelling Mongols ruled the largest empire in human history, which stretched a quarter of the way around the planet and encompassed half of the world's population.

Put Him on a Plane (Part 3)

On Thursday, September 14, at 8:00 p.m. on the dot, our precious neighbor, Mike, pulled up in front of our house, and we began the intense process of loading Smoke, Gerdie, their tack and hay, plus my luggage, into his truck and trailer. I was so exhausted, both mentally and physically, that I was simply functioning on autopilot. The boxes and luggage went into a closed compartment in the trailer. The hay was stowed in the truck bed. Then, Smoke and Gerdie were walked through our dark pasture and into the trailer. My heart was pounding out of my chest as I hugged Pat good-bye, whispering that I would see him in three days. (He was staying behind to finish closing up our mostly empty home.)

Mike was the perfect person to shuttle us to LAX. His calm, steadfast demeanor helped to quiet my frantic heart and mind. By the time we made it down the mountain, I was starting to breathe normally, and the throbbing in my temples had subsided. We reminisced of our years as neighbors, and I shared with him the hopes and dreams Pat and I held for our future in paradise. I also felt comfortable in revealing how concerned I was in putting Smoke on the cargo plane. He was a large horse, and I wasn't sure I could handle unloading him from the trailer and walking him up to the loading zone. Mike said he would handle that, and I was not to worry! It was so reassuring to talk through all that was directly ahead of us, knowing that God was ultimately in total control and had provided help during my time of need. Then, the third bomb of our journey dropped.

I was instructed many times by Andee, the Pacific Airlift representative, to "be at the loading zone at 11:00 p.m., not early, and certainly not late." So that is exactly what we did. As we pulled up, there they were, stretched before us—enormous cargo planes in various stages of loading and unloading. I immediately started to panic, envisioning Smoke breaking loose and wildly running onto the airport runway! Mike had different thoughts. He suggested I find the check-in area while he stayed with the animals. "Good idea," I croaked. It took me a few minutes to locate the narrow walkway leading to the Pacific Airlift Cargo Office. When I approached the desk and provided my name, the representative said, "You're too early! We don't load until 1:00 a.m."

"Really? I was specifically instructed to be here at 11:00 p.m."

"Well, we will come and get you when we're ready" was his burly reply. I took a few deep breaths and walked back to Mike, making my report.

"No problem. We'll just sit tight." Then, 1:00 a.m. came and went, along with 2:00 a.m. and 3:00 a.m. Smoke and Gerdie had to remain in the trailer for safety purposes. Around 3:30 a.m., a mechanic found us and reported that they had a little "problem" with the aircraft, but it would be repaired soon. What? A little problem with the aircraft? I quickly increased my silent prayers, while Mike just smiled and suggested I take a nap. Yeah, right! Meanwhile, other weary travelers of the four-legged persuasion arrived. Smoke would have friends on the trip. At 5:00 a.m., a full six hours after pulling up to the "Cargo Drop Off" area, Smoke and Gerdie took a short walk from the trailer, up a narrow ramp, and into the three-part compartment that would be their home for the next thirteen hours. (They would fly to Honolulu with a veterinary technician, as well as our assorted boxes and container of tack. Upon arrival in Honolulu, they would be rolled off the plane, inspected by a USDA agent, and then rolled back on to the plane for their inter-island trip to Kailua-Kona Airport. Upon arrival in Kona, they would be rolled off and then pulled by tractor to a pre-designated pick-up area. It was all way over my head.)

Very quickly, we were ushered out of the loading area as the doors were pulled closed. You could have pushed me over with a feather. My beloved equine friend of twenty-three years was now in the hands of complete strangers. And the entire experience, thus far, did anything but provide me with the assurance that I would see Smoke and Gerdie later that day!

By the time Mike escorted me through the hotel lobby and confirmed my check-in at the reception desk, I had a scant hour and fifteen minutes before catching the shuttle for my own flight to Hawaii. No time for a nap, I reasoned. Pitching my luggage on the bed, I filled the tub with hot water and did the "Calgon, take me away!" soak. It was heaven on earth. After a thirty-minute respite, I threw on clean clothes, brushed my hair and teeth, grabbed an apple as the hostess was setting up the continental breakfast bar in the lobby, and stumbled onto the shuttle. Miraculously, I made it on to my designated flight and in to my designated seat. Is this really happening, or am I dreaming? You would think that once I was in the air I would pass out from exhaustion, not only due to the emotional roller coaster of the past eighteen hours, but because it had been twenty-four hours since I had slept. But sleep would not come. My mind simply would not shut down.

I was leaving my home, my city, my state, my family, and my friends. My horse and goat were flying what I hoped were the friendly skies. We would be living with new friends for a month, then moving to a rented yurt. (I didn't even know what a yurt was four years ago!) Within a month, I would fly back to California for our oldest daughter's wedding. The following day, we would send our only son off to Coast Guard Boot Camp in New Jersey, then board a plane back to Hawaii. *Is this really happening, or am I dreaming? "Yes! And I will be with you every step of the way." "Thank you, Jesus!"* was my inward reply.

Five and a half hours after leaving the runway at LAX, our wheels touched down safely at Kailua-Kona Airport. Adrenalin was pumping through my veins as I strained to locate Karen and John's truck and trailer. Graciously, they had agreed to make the five-hour roundtrip to collect Smoke, Gerdie, myself, and all our paraphernalia, and then shuttle us back to their twenty-acre ranch. Spotting them brought tears to my bloodshot eyes. After almost collapsing into their outstretched arms, Karen placed a bright orange lei around my neck, giving me the customary aloha welcome—a gentle hug and a kiss on the cheek. I was home. Then, the fourth bomb dropped.

I didn't have a clue as to how or where we would collect Smoke and Gerdie. Thankfully, John had done his research and knew the location of the drop-off—a private asphalt road located in the middle of a volcanic lava rock field slightly off the airport. After locating the road, we decided to make a quick trip to a convenience store for cold drinks. It was 1:00 p.m. and at least ninety-five degrees. By the time we returned, over a dozen stock trailers had assembled along the side of the road…packed with burros! In addition, there were dozens of parked cars and people milling around, many toting clipboards and cameras.

"John, what is going on?" I asked. He calmly explained that the island boasts a large herd of wild burros called the Waikoloa Nightingales. The herd had expanded to the point where the land could not sustain them. So 119 had been rounded up and would be loaded onto the very cargo plane that Smoke and Gerdie were to exit. They would then be transported to a burro refuge located in Texas. (I had actually read the story while flying over just a few short hours earlier. I just didn't realize they would become Smoke and Gerdie's welcome party!) The magazine article explained the amazing effort this burro rescue required on behalf of the Hawaii Humane Society, the island's premier veterinarian, Dr. Brady Bergin, and dozens of volunteers. Then it hit me like a ton of bricks—Smoke and Gerdie would be required to disembark in the midst of all this hoopla!

My heart began to race as I tried to imagine how Smoke would respond when he heard, saw, and took a whiff of what I was looking at. Panic began to rise up in every fiber of my being. Almost three hours after the intended arrival time, I heard someone shout, "Here they come!" Standing on my tiptoes, I peered above the crowd in front of me, and down the hot asphalt road, to see Smoke's Palomino head peeking out over the rails that had served as his stall for the past eighteen hours. Keeping my tears in check, I pushed through the throng of Nightingale supporters and watched as he and Gerdie were pulled to a stop a few feet away. Carefully, the gate was lowered, and then the vet tech slowly guided Smoke down the ramp. People cheered and cameras clicked as I grabbed the lead rope and walked Smoke toward the waiting trailer. (Thankfully, Karen took control of Gerdie!) One of the many journalists documenting the transport of the burros asked for a quick interview and photo. We obliged. Then we walked up the ramp and into John's trailer, securing both animals for the final leg of their amazing journey. What an event!

Two and a half hours later, I walked Smoke into his new temporary stall, gave him a kiss on his soft pink muzzle, put Gerdie into the pasture, and collapsed into bed. We made it! Unbelievably and against all odds, we made it! Three and a half years of dreaming, seven weeks of fast-track packing, twenty-one hours of travel, and we were finally here. I prayed another prayer of thanksgiving to my heavenly Father, vowing that I would never do this again!

> The Lord is my shepherd, I shall not want. He makes me lie down in green pastures; He leads me beside quiet waters. He restores my soul; He guides me in the paths of righteousness for His name's sake. Even though I walk through the valley of the shadow of death, I fear no evil; for Thou art with me; Thy rod and Thy staff, they comfort me. Thou dost prepare a table before me in the presence of my enemies; Thou hast anointed my head with oil; my cup overflows. Surely goodness and lovingkindness will follow me all the days of my life, and I will dwell in the house of the Lord forever.
>
> Psalm 23

The four bombs that dropped as Smoke, Gerdie, and I journeyed from Big Bear, California, to the Hamakua Coast of Hawaii took me by surprise. But they were no surprise to my heavenly Father. He knew all about them! And He cleared the way, every step of the way. He provided just enough time for me to pack up and leave a full twenty-four hours ahead of schedule! He provided kind friends and strangers to join us along the way. And it was His heavenly angels that delivered us safely. When we are in the midst of a remarkable journey, it isn't often clear how God is orchestrating the details, both monumental as well as minute. But upon reflection, it is easy to see His loving hands at work. Evidence of His work is all around us. All we need to do is open our hearts, ears, and eyes to recognize Him. If God cares about the tiny sparrow, how much more does He care about you and me?

Thank You, Lord, for hearing my frantic prayers, for bringing my twenty-nine-year-old equine friend with me to Hawaii so that his elderly lips could graze in the lush green grass of this beautiful island, spending his final days, weeks, months, and hopefully, years doing what horses were made to do. Thank You for lovingly going before us, preparing the way for a safe arrival. And thank You that no matter where I go, You are there. In Jesus's name, amen.

YURT FACTOID:

Cart houses were used both in war and peacetime. Their yurt-like frames rested on a bottom wooden ring that allowed them to extend out beyond the cart's two wheels by as much as five feet on either side. The tents were not collapsible, but the entire tent could be lifted off the cart and placed on the ground. A thirteenth-century account described a cart so large (twenty feet in diameter) that it took two rows of eleven oxen each to pull the cart.

One Plus One Equals...Three!

One of my first introductions to animal husbandry came in the form of caring for a neighbor's milking goats while they took a much-deserved family vacation. I was about ten years old, and we had recently put down stakes in the rural community of Yorba Linda, California. I had never been in the presence of goats, let alone understood the process of grabbing their teats and somehow extracting a steady flow of the white stuff. After a series of introductory instructions, I finally passed the test and, once or twice a year, found myself at the soft side of a dozen Nubians, gently tugging on teats, filling the pails, and storing the precious liquid. Each job paid twenty-five dollars, a fortune for this budding entrepreneur! These periodic teat-tugging episodes led me to eventual ownership of my own Nubian goat. My mom named him Flicker due to the silver flecks of hair that stood out against a backdrop of charcoal on his floppy ears and Roman nose head. I don't remember the birthing, just the joy of bringing home the weaned four-legged creature, falling more deeply in love with him every day.

My parents divorced when I was sixteen years old. This eventually created a situation whereby Flicker and two of our three horses went off to new homes. To say this was painful would be a gross understatement. My animals were my life! As I entered my twenties, thirties, and early forties, I held tightly to the dream of once again enjoying the friendship of a goat. But it wasn't until I had married Pat in 2001, moving my horse, Smoke, and myself to the mountain community of Big Bear, California, that my dream had any chance of becoming a reality. By the time our second anniversary rolled around, we had purchased a one-acre lot, complete with majestic Jeffrey pine and Cypress trees, plus spectacular mountain views. By our fourth anniversary, we were settled into our three-thousand-square-foot home of our dreams, boasting a 32' × 36' MD Barn in the backyard. My two twelve-year-old bonus daughters, Lindsey and Nicole, were equally anxious to add at least one Nubian goat to our barnyard mix.

In addition to my lifelong love for this breed, Nubians make great stable mates for horses. Since Smoke was the only equine on the property, I felt he could use a friend. One sunny afternoon, we took a short drive to visit our friend's neighborhood petting zoo. Kay was famous for providing many of the backyard critters in our area, including llamas, potbelly pigs, ponies, chickens, and goats. After careful consideration, we welcomed four-month-old Tinkerbelle, a Nubian, and two-month- old, Annabelle, a Nigerian Dwarf, into our family. (Goats, like horses, cattle, and sheep are herding animals. They do best when they have friends of the same animal persuasion.) Now, Lindsey and Nicole could experience the same joy I had known as a young girl, times two! Five years later, we had a brainstorm. We decided that it would be a wonderful experience to breed Tinkerbelle. Her personality was so loving we felt she would make an excellent mother. Little did we know.

One May afternoon, Pat and I walked Tinkerbelle down the street to our neighbor's ranch whereby she was repeatedly violated by their male goat. We visited her a few times during the process, receiving encouragement by the owner that she was surely impregnated! Poor Tinkerbelle. She didn't have the glow of upcoming motherhood! Hmm…five weeks later, excited about the potential birth sometime in October, we walked her back to her own barnyard, which now included Zoe, a potbelly pig, and four assorted chickens. Lo and behold, five and a half months later, Tinkerbelle looked like she was about to explode! Poor Tinkerbelle. (Again!) Her udder was so swollen we thought it would burst. Her enormous belly swayed from side to side as she carefully made her way around her paddock. *How many kids are in there?* we wondered to ourselves. When it appeared she could go no further, I set my alarm clock to check on her in the middle of the night. Nothing.

So I reset my alarm and got up early the next morning. I found her lying on a fresh bed of shavings in her cozy shed, refusing to get up. I could see that her water had broken. Other than a sorrowful look in her deep brown eyes, she seemed fine. I quickly ran back into the house, up the stairs, and into our bedroom. "Tinkerbelle is about to give birth!" I shouted to Pat as I grabbed his shoulder to shake him awake.

He turned over, opened one eye, and said, "Wake me when the baby is born."

"What? Are you kidding? Come on. Get up! I need some help here!" And I ran out the bedroom door. Keep in mind that I had never witnessed the birth of a goat kid. Kittens were about all I could refer to.

Shortly after I positioned myself in the corner of the shed, Tinkerbelle rolled completely onto her side, made a few murmurs, and out popped a kid! She soon did what all good goat mothers do— she leaned over to inspect, clean, and snuggle her newborn. How adorable the infant was. Her gray fur matted with moisture from the birth, those long spindly legs, and a matching set of brown eyes that seemed to say, "Where am I?" We had decided months earlier that if we got a girl, her name was to be Sister Bertrille. Do you remember the popular late 1960s TV series *The Flying Nun* staring Sally Field? If so, you can't forget the funky white head covering worn by the quirkiest nun the San Tanco, Puerto Rico, convent had ever witnessed. That headgear resembled enormous wings that made this tiny nun seem just steps away from takeoff; sort of like a Nubian's ears!

As I monitored the newborn, I noticed that Tinkerbelle did not get up and move around. And her tummy was still huge. We were told that first-time mothers usually produce one kid but in future pregnancies can deliver two, sometimes three kids. Did Tinkerbelle have another little gift waiting to be birthed? We waited…and we waited, and we waited.

Almost a full hour later, she repeated her little moan, rolled onto her side, gave a good push, and out came infant number 2! We were amazed—a little brown and white girl. Two girls! We were thrilled. Tinkerbelle was less than thrilled. She pretty much ignored this newest member of her family, refusing to lick her clean or even snuggle with her. *Now what?* Pat had shown up by that time and quickly removed the birthing sack that covered part of her face and nose. We massaged her and spoke loving words to her. Sister Bertrille, now one hour old, was wobbling around trying to nurse her mother. But number 2, not yet named, just lay there. So I dashed to the phone and called the ranch where we had had Tinker bred, asking them to "come quickly and take a look." Within ten minutes, our neighbor's car screeched to a halt in our driveway.

They ran through the gate and up to the small animal paddock. It was quickly noted that Tinkerbelle was not allowing Sister Bertrille to nurse. We tried everything, but she refused. To have any chance of survival, these babies had to receive the all-important colostrum that is initially produced in the milk. And number 2 had to stand up! Our neighbor cross-tied Tinker using two lead ropes. Then, with a few rough tugs, he was able to get her milk flowing. We tried to help Sister Bertrille "hook up," but Tinkerbelle made such a ruckus, kicking at the little thing and moving around constantly. At that point, my maternal instincts and youthful training kicked into gear. I saddled up next to Tink and began the process of extracting the valuable milk into baby bottles provided by our neighbors. She did not like this one tiny bit. But I was bound and determined to keep these babies alive, with or without her help! So much for being a good mother! That responsibility now shifted to me.

Crouching next to Tinkerbelle and tugging on her engorged teats brought back such tender memories of my childhood. I just loved the whole process. Forget the fact that we didn't do the math, and she gave birth in October during the biggest winter snowstorm the San Bernardino Mountains had seen in over thirty years! And talk about work. Initially, the babies had to eat every two hours. Every two hours! Then over the next four-month period, we slowly cut back to every four hours, then every six hours, then finally twice daily. I was, of course, the designated milker, strainer, and bottle feeder come rain, shine, hail, or snowstorm. Eventually, we had to move the little family into the breezeway of our barn because the snow had grown to over four feet in depth! What an event. But I have to say that it was well worth it. The babies were happy, healthy, and, as promised, provided a steady flow of footloose and fancy-free entertainment.

PS: Pat took on the responsibility of naming number 2. That was a big mistake. He insisted on calling her Gertrude. Come on! Really? We lovingly nicknamed her Gerdie, which he insisted rhymed well with Bertie, Sister Bertrille's nickname. And even though both goats had a rough start, Gerdie turned out to be the most wonderfully good-natured goat of all! Now, find out how Gerdie got to Hawaii, and the surprise blessing we all received once we arrived. Here's a tip: It pays to be a good goat!

> Every good thing bestowed and every perfect gift is from above, coming down from the Father of lights, with whom there is no variation, or shifting shadow. James 1:17

YURT FACTOID:

Yurts are one of the oldest forms of indigenous shelters, still used today by nomads from Turkey to Mongolia.

Our house in Big Bear, CA

Smoke and Jen heading out in Big Bear

Mr. & Mrs. Greg Christman – Married October 22, 2011

Christopher Burke and Jen
U.S.C.G. Boot Camp Graduation – December 16, 2011

A very pregnant Tinkerbelle!

Tinkerbell with Twins -
Gertrude (Gerdie) and Sister Bertrille (Bertie)

Smoke exiting his tiny cargo stall
at the Kailua-Kona Airport

Season One

November 2011

–

January 2012

Heidi

Goats are similar to dogs, only better! They will stay in your yard, trim the weeds (and flower gardens if left unattended), and even walk with you down a country road. Their friendly, loving nature is so endearing and entertaining! What a barrel of laughs watching them leap straight into the air and then hip-hop sideways as they dance around your yard. They have so much energy they simply don't know what to do with it!

When we were given the spiritual green light to finally move to the Big Island, and received the contract to fly our horse and three goats over, we were forced to make the painful decision to leave Tinkerbelle and Bertie with our friends, the Geigers. (By this time, Annabelle, the Nigerian Dwarf goat, and Zoe, the potbelly pig, were long gone. They had not acclimated well to the babies, and we feared for their little lives. So off they went to new homes.) Three thousand dollars to fly three goats pushed us beyond our already meager moving budget. And this mother-daughter team helped to fulfill the Geiger's dream of goat ownership.

Although Tinkerbelle never fully bonded with either of her twin daughters, she tolerated Sister Bertille, while headbutting poor Gerdie all over their paddock. In self-defense, Gerdie ended up spending much of her time on top of a huge cable spool. So when we were forced to choose, Gerdie was the only one to receive her flight wings. It pays to be a good goat!

Shortly after arriving at the twenty-acre ranch of our friends, John and Karen, and getting Smoke and Gerdie settled into their temporary paddocks, we were introduced to Heidi. John and Karen's ranch sports six horses, approximately three dozen sheep, two dogs, and a number of felines.

"What are you doing with a two-week-old goat kid," I asked as Karen gave me the tour. This tiny animal stood out like a sore thumb when compared to the other barnyard pets. They explained that a nearby neighbor had found both her and her brother in another neighbor's field. The mother was nowhere to be found, and the owners were off island. These babies had been abandoned, and the brother had died a day or two after they were given to John and Karen. With no mother in sight, they were bottle-feeding this little one right along with three newborn lambs that were not receiving the kind of attention they needed from their mothers! (What's up with all these mothers?) It was a barnyard nursery, for sure. I asked what her name was, and Karen said they called her Heidi, named after the endearing children's story of the same title. It fit her to a tee. Heidi seemed totally oblivious to the fact that she didn't look remotely like the baby lambs she shared quarters with. She just seemed grateful to be alive!

Two weeks after we began our one-month stay with John and Karen, and as I popped yet another baby bottle of lamb formula into Heidi's expectant mouth, I asked Karen if they intended to add to their fledgling goat herd. Her calm reply? "No. We're giving Heidi to you guys!" I practically dropped the bottle as I wondered what Pat would think about this new tidbit of information. Gerdie was bonding with Heidi, and they really *were* adorable girlfriends. Even though Heidi was only one-month-old, she ran the "kindergarten," as Pat liked to refer to that area of the ranch. So we were now the proud owners of one Nubian and one "motley," as we jokingly referred to the newest member of the McGeehan herd.

When we left our home in Big Bear, we not only said good-bye to family, friends, and our beautiful home, we had to say good-bye to three family members of the creature kind—our gray seal point kitty, Chloe, who we left with a friend while she was waiting to clear her titer test, and two of our three goats, Tinkerbelle and Sister Bertrille. It was painful, and we missed their precious faces and adorable antics. God knew all about the pain we felt. The surprising announcement from Karen that they were giving Heidi to us was His first step in restoring what we had lost during the move.

After our brief stay at the ranch, we moved into our tiny rented yurt in Paauilo, where two additional pets were soon to be added to our "herd." God, in His grace and mercy, replaced Chloe with a starving, coal-black feline we named Mauka. (Mauka translated is "upcountry" in Hawaiian.) Then, we welcomed Makai, which means "seaward," an adorable orange female tabby kitten. What a blessing these "girls" have been to our little yurt experience, serving as continued confirmation that God truly does restore what is lost or stolen. He does this when we trust Him to care for our every need. In our humanness, it seems impossible that the Creator of the universe would have the time or the interest to care about what seems to be the "little things" of our lives. After all, doesn't world hunger demand more of His attention? I sure don't have all the answers, except to say that time and time again, God has proven His faithfulness in returning to me what this world has taken.

This time, it was in the form of one tiny goat kid named Heidi.

> Then I will make up to you for the years that the swarming locust has eaten.
>
> Joel 2:25a

YURT FACTOID:

While there are many small differences in yurt design as you move from tribe to tribe across the high, dry country of Central Asia, the basic design remains the same: a portable dwelling consisting of a folding lattice wall and radial roof poles set in a skylight rim, all held together with a tension band at the eaves and the hole covered with thick blankets of wool felt.

William Coperthwaite

Healing from the Ground Up

Loyalty is a quality I find very appealing. My oldest daughter, Ashley, is extremely loyal, always going to bat for me when the chips are down. Pat is the premier example of the loyal hubby, taking to heart the words spoken to us at a Presbytery Conference shortly after we married. "Never speak negatively about your spouse. Be each other's encouragers." (Truth be told, I have forgotten those sage words of advice on one too many occasions!)

As the grateful recipient of Ashley and Pat's loyalty, my heart's desire is to provide an equal measure of loyalty to them, as well as everyone I love, including my faithful equine. Smoke and I have been partners for over twenty-three years. He filled a huge void created years earlier when my parents divorced and I was forced to sell my two beautiful quarter horses, tack and all. Those years of simply watching horses graze in nearby pastures often caused tears to slowly fill my eyes. Fifteen years passed before I was in a position to be able to purchase, stable, and maintain another animal of this size.

Smoke was the last horse I considered in a long line of test rides. By the time I found him advertised in a horse publication, I was exhausted from driving all over heaven's green earth, only to be disappointed when each horse failed my evaluation test. One ran off with me. Another had terrible confirmation. No emotional connection. Small eyes. Wrong color. But I reluctantly called the number on the ad, asking the owner to bring him to me. Victorville was a good three-hour drive, and I just couldn't muster the strength to travel that far. Surprisingly, the owner agreed!

I wouldn't go so far as to say that, for me, it was love at first sight as Smoke slowly backed out of the trailer. My heart was set on a deep golden Palomino, just like Coppertone, my unbeatable trail class winner. Although Smoke was a lighter Palomino, he had the size of sixteen and a half hands, the right age (seven years old), excellent confirmation, and offered a very comfortable ride—smooth as glass at the trot and canter. He was also a registered Appaloosa, boasting an interesting blanket of white spots on his rear. These, I loving refer to now as polka dots. This horse possessed one additional quality—large, expressive eyes, eyes that seemed to draw me into the very depths of his soul. I told the owner I would think about it and call her in a day or two. Then, an interesting thing happened as she attempted to load him back into the trailer. He refused to load! Smoke was a show horse, so he was more than familiar with the load, unload, load procedure. But try as she might, she could not get him in! A full half hour later, I finally said, "Just leave him with me. I will get him vet checked, and if he passes, I'll buy him." She agreed. And as they say, "The rest is history!"

Smoke and I have been through more than our fair share of excitement. At sixteen years old, he had coliced. There are many reasons why a horse will colic. But the bottom line is they cannot pass their stools. They stop eating, and they will die if the cause is not identified and rectified within a very short period. After two visits from my local vet, and only temporary improvement on Smoke's part, we determined that he had to take a trip to the Chino Hills Equine Hospital. Nine X-rays later revealed three huge stones in his abdomen—ten pounds of stones! These stones are similar to kidney stones in a human being, but a heck of a lot bigger! And passing these monsters were completely out of the question. The surgeon met with me in the waiting room and gave me our options: 75 percent survival with the operation, certain death without. At that moment, I was so thankful I had equine insurance covering 80 percent of his medical expenses.

"Let's go for it," I croaked through my tears.

Smoke made it through this major surgical procedure and three-month recovery. Soon, we were once again saddling up to ride the hills of Orange Park Acres.

The next twelve years were problem-free. During that time, Pat and I married, and Smoke found himself enjoying weekly rides through the San Bernardino National Forest. What a blessing it was to explore mountain trails after a winter snowstorm that left six to eight inches of white fluffy powder. The stillness of this winter wonderland created extended times of deep reflection and gratitude for the life I was blessed with—good health, a strong Christian marriage, wonderful kids, a satisfying job, excellent church, loving extended family and friends, as well as a unique relationship with one of God's finest creatures. Then, disaster struck…

It was a hot August Sunday in 2010. Smoke and I had just received the Hi Point ribbon, winning first place in most of our classes at the Los Vaqueros De La Montana Riding Club's Western Horse Show. On Monday, my farrier, Craig, came out to trim Smoke's hooves and give him a new set of horseshoes. On Tuesday morning, I discovered Smoke limping as he meandered between his stall and attached turnout. I will spare you the gory details and just say that after three long weeks of extensive investigation by two additional farriers and our local vet, Smoke was transferred to the same equine hospital and surgeon who had saved his life twelve years earlier. After a full set of X-rays, I was told he had suffered a coffin bone rotation on his right front hoof. Imagine your anklebone crashing through the sole of your foot, and you get the idea!

After exhaustive conversations with the surgeon, I privately asked Craig for his opinion. His answer sent me into the stratosphere. "Of the seventeen horses I have cared for over the past fifteen years who have been diagnosed with this extreme trauma, none have survived. I would put him down." I felt as though I would faint as the reality of Smoke's condition sunk into my heart, soul, and mind. My friend of over twenty-one years, the one who depended on me for his care, now faced a life-threatening fork in his trail. What was I to do? Allow me to skip to the end.

After one full year of exhaustive rehabilitation, a $10,000 medical investment including a six-week hospital stay, a complete dietary change, medications, supplements, an unexpected surgical procedure, special orthotic boots, and a ton of prayer and love, Smoke and I once again saddled up to ride our local mountain trails. It was a day I will never forget, filled with a nonstop stream of thankful tears. Together, we had beaten the odds, said no to the easiest way out, listened to the divinely inspired advice of my farrier's wife, done our research, and allowed the process of healing to have its way.

I often wonder if somehow, someway, Smoke sensed twenty-one years earlier that he would not once, but twice, need his caregiver to demonstrate 100 percent loyalty to him, someone who would place his emergency needs at the very top of her list, sacrificing her time and limited financial resources to demonstrate that every once in a while, the impossible *is* possible? Is this the real reason he refused to load back into his trailer? I really wonder…

Once the decision was made to move to Hawaii, my concerns shifted to Smoke and the special care he would require for the rest of his life. By this time, I had made the decision to allow him to return to the way God had created equines to exist—barefoot—meaning no metal shoes nailed to their hooves. But finding a qualified, highly trained barefoot farrier on the Big Island would be similar to trying to locate a single quarter, painted with bright red nail polish, and then thrown into a sea of quarters within an area the size of Texas! What were the chances? With God, the impossible *is* possible. Within four weeks of arriving in Hawaii, I had been divinely guided to Susanella. I lovingly refer to her as "the world's finest barefoot farrier." What a plethora of equine knowledge. What a lover of all sizes, shapes, breeds, and conditions of this majestic animal.

The first time we met, we both talked so fast it made our heads spin. Quickly, we realized we were on the same page regarding Smoke's continued physical needs. She basically tucked us under her maternal wing, providing the painstaking care that, over the next year, would result in beautifully restored and functioning hooves, "Healing from the ground up" as she so often refers to her meticulous work. The fact that we are the same age, A-type personalities, and totally committed to the care of our equine friends has made this sometimes frightening journey so much more enjoyable. Susanella is more than my farrier. She is my dear friend, confidant of all things equine, and the one I call when Smoke and I need help!

On April 28, 2012, we celebrated Smoke's thirtieth birthday—the equivalent of eighty-six and a half human years. I felt he deserved it after all he has been through in his adventurous lifetime. I inserted fragrant ginger into his braided forelock, mane and tail, tying a bright orange lei around his beautiful neck. Susanella, along with a dozen neighbors and friends, stopped by to enjoy pupus and champagne while sitting on hay bales scattered near Smoke's pasture. We all marveled at this amazing example of equine flesh. But I knew Who truly healed my horse, the Great Physician, the only One who not only healed the lepers, raised Lazarus after four days in his grave, stopped a woman's flow of blood after twelve years, caused the deaf to hear, the blind to see, and the lame to walk, but also rose from His own grave, fellowshipped among the multitudes, and then ascended back to heaven to be seated at the right hand of His heavenly Father. Jesus Christ heard my panic prayers and chose again to answer yes, giving Smoke and me an untold number of additional years together to enjoy life on the Big Island. We are truly blessed!

> And hearing this, Jesus said to them, "It is not those who are healthy who need a physician, but those who are sick; I did not come to call the righteous, but sinners."
>
> Mark 2:17

YURT FACTOID:

Bill Coperthwaite calls his place and his work the Yurt Foundation, which is fitting. It is because of Bill that yurts migrated to the west. Bill established the Yurt Foundation in 1992 to continue exploring and sharing his vision of blending wisdom from various cultures, ancient and modern, to invent simpler, more harmonious, and more "democratic" ways of living.

Bathroom 101

I can't remember the exact moment I became the "Calgon, take me away!" poster woman. Chances are the transformation occurred during the crazy years of raising two kiddos while working half to full time…from home! There is something so very soothing about soaking in a vintage white enamel and iron bathtub, with nothing but a good novel or *People* magazine to occupy my overworked mind and body. Pat understands my bathtub thing and was particularly sympathetic when we both realized that the yurt accommodations included a bathroom…but *no* bathtub. As shock registered all over my face, he quickly assured me that we could "add a tub outside, under the Ohia tree." That seemed doable. Soon, we were, in our mind's eye, creating a cozy and private nook for my daily soaking pleasure.

Prior to beginning the bathtub project, another project demanded my most immediate attention—the bathroom. This 6' × 7' tiled enclosure, located outside the yurt, down the lava rock pathway, and under the lanai, boasted a toilet, a small pedestal sink, a shower head, and a medicine chest that looked like it had hitched a ride on the Mayflower! The pièce de résistance was the moss-covered entrance door, which measured a full three inches too wide, included a gapping two-inch hole where the door handle should have been, and a rusty hook for closure purposes.

Our one and only bathroom did offer a window but no method of providing privacy. The portions of wall that were not tiled, as well as the ceiling, were a rust-speckled shade of dingy white. Let's not discuss the condition of the grout.

It was common knowledge that Bailey, our Hawaii realtor, and his wife, Baki, had successfully raised their family of four children while living in this yurt. And a family of five had recently moved into their new home after renting it for five months. So what was up with this dysfunctional bathroom? I guess dysfunctional is in the eye of the beholder…or the decorator. My mind went into overdrive as I tried to figure out how to improve the situation…and fast!

Refusing to get frustrated over my new bathroom, I spent hours drumming up creative ways to solve the problematic areas. Paint was an obvious first step. The wall tiles offered a combination of white and hunter green, with white and tan tiles on the floor. So I selected a muted hue of green for the walls, a slightly darker green for the lovely door and door jams, and gloss white for the ceiling. Bye-bye, rust stains. After two failed attempts, we found a three-door white medicine cabinet that successfully covered the gaping whole where the vintage version once hung.

My biggest design challenge came in creating a shower curtain program that would provide privacy as well as help to contain the shower overspray that otherwise sprinkled everything within the space. The answer came in suspending two black curtain rods from the ceiling rather than the walls, as is customary. I selected two opaque shower curtains sporting an image of bamboo that, when slid closed at the far corner, successfully kept the water in, and the eyes of any Peeping Tom out! Aside from the medicine cabinet, no shelving or storage area was provided to hold our personal items. To take care of this challenge, I located two small shelves that had made the trip from Big Bear, gave them a fresh coat of glossy black paint, and placed one above the toilet, and the other to the left of the tiny sink. A plastic three-drawer cabinet, nestled between the toilet and the shower area, solved the storage problem.

The yurt is located in such a rural area that privacy isn't an issue for us. But on behalf of our occasional and less than adventuresome visitors, I suspended from a delicate black curtain rod, my favorite piece of vintage floral fabric found on a Santa Barbara, California, shopping excursion years earlier. I embellished each end with a matching black-beaded tassel given to me by my dear friend, Myrna, three houses back. A scrap of light-gray satin ribbon gathering the fabric at the center point created a stunning, or at least eye-pleasing, window presentation. The vintage white metal magazine rack, nailed over an area where the dry wall was pealing, finished that particular wall.

Just prior to exiting Big Bear, I stumbled upon a vintage pair of bamboo-framed Hawaiian prints of the flora persuasion. I needed them like a hole in the head, but I just couldn't resist. I confiscated one of the two that I had hung in the yurt, and it found its temporary new home above the toilet. Things were really shaping up!

Now for the door issue. After a serious scrubbing, the original door received two coats of darker green paint. (I knew this was a temporary fix.) Over the next two weeks, excessive discussion ensued as we considered our best replacement door option. We measured and calculated this unusual opening, noting the land mines on all four sides: the cement stoop would need to be lowered, an overhang needed to be cleared, which way the door should open, window or no window, unpainted or prepainted? After two unsuccessful installation attempts, the third time was the charm. We finally settled on a white metal, prepainted door, complete with slider window, opening in (conveniently blocking access to the light switch!) with a threshold that kept the rain and most of the Ohia leaves outside; although the ants still found their way in! And voilà, the bathroom not only worked, it looked beautiful! I secretly mused as to the possibility of uploading a few "before and after" pictures to *House Beautiful* magazine. Then, I scratched that notion, deciding that beauty truly is in the eye of the beholder.

Our shower experience in this bathroom is anything but ordinary. So I developed what I lovingly refer to as the "Proper Shower Procedure." Here is how it goes:

1. Enter the new and improved bathroom, closing the door behind you.
2. Pick up and fold the woven floor mat, slipping it between the left wall and the toilet.
3. Move the green bucket from under the dripping showerhead to the opposite side of the bathroom. If you feel like it, dump the water outside under a plant.

4. Strip, carefully placing your clothing on top of the plastic storage cabinet.
5. Push the showerhead to the right, facing the wall. This helps to keep the sink from receiving unnecessary overspray.
6. Turn the water knob all the way to the left until the scalding hot water finds its way out the head. Slowly adjust to the desired temperature and reposition the shower head.
7. Step inside the 3' × 3' space, closing the two curtains so they meet in the far corner. (No yanking, please!)
8. Scrub-a-dub-dub to your heart's content or until the hot water runs out.
9. Off goes the water. Back goes the curtains.
10. Dry off, hanging your towel back on the "towel" bar.
11. Take a firm grip on the long handle of the squeegee, and scrape all excess water into the shower drain.
12. Grab the roll of paper towels located behind the toilet. Make a wad of seven or eight sections, throwing it on the floor. Then, use your foot to complete the final water mop-up.
13. Place the green bucket back under the shower head and the mat in front of the door.
14. Apply all necessary lotions and potions. Dress. Or, in Pat's case, run, buck naked, back into the yurt.

And there you have it—the "Proper Shower Procedure!" Now try explaining or demonstrating that one to a courageous friend or family member visiting from the mainland.

The unveiling of the bathroom, minus the "Proper Shower Procedure", occurred on December 25 during our Christmas open-yurt party. This was our first Christmas off the mainland, with no family to join us in celebrating the arrival of the Christ Child over two thousand years ago. So, as is often the Hawaiian custom, we invited our island ohana—our local family—to stop by between the hours of 1:00 and 4:00 p.m. Although Bailey had marveled at the interior furnishings of the yurt, neither he nor his family had seen the ugly duckling transformation of the bathroom. Watching their eyes pop open warmed my heart, while providing a great source of entertainment and encouragement. Frankly, I loved the whole process. And I appreciated Bailey's and Baki's willingness to absorb all costs associated with the DIY improvement.

Initially, the adjustment to yurt living occurred little by little. For me, the biggest challenge has been the bathroom. But I have to admit it has been a true blessing in so many ways. This little nook has served us well: as a nursery when our tiny orange tabby kitten, Makai, was adjusting to her new home, and as a satellite office during the wee hours of early morning as Pat tries to snatch a few more precious hours of sleep, but I need to call my family, friends, or editor. And as Pat often says, "It has the best view while sitting on the throne." And what about Pat's promise of the bathtub addition? He is one to keep his promises, so I will wait patiently and see what happens. Meanwhile, the warm ocean waters surrounding my new Hawaii home will just have to do!

> Wash me thoroughly from my iniquity and cleanse me from my sin.
>
> Psalm 51:2

YURT FACTOID:

Pastoral nomads traditionally move through four seasonal encampments (winter, spring, summer, and fall); though, the time spent in each varies from a few weeks to many months.

Don't Judge a Book
by Its Cover

When you relocate, especially from Mainland United States to the Big Island, the challenge of finding a new family physician, dentist, and ophthalmologist can be a daunting task. (About as exciting as knowing you have to schedule a colonoscopy!) It was also necessary for us to secure a new insurance company. Doesn't that sound like fun?

After making a minimum of twenty inquiry phone calls to family physicians on our provider list, we had come up with a big fat zero. "We are sorry, but we are not accepting new patients at this time," was the anthem we repetitively heard from the other end of the phone line. So we called our new insurance company, moving up the chain of command, and finally, announced to some poor soul, "If you don't find us a physician, we are canceling our policy *and* demanding a full refund!"

A few days later, we had two names and phone numbers. Pat called the first one on the list, and before you could say, "Mamalahoa Highway," we had dual appointments to meet Dr. David A. Jung. (I called the second suggested physician just for the fun of it but ultimately received the same "anthem.") The receptionist kindly explained to me what the problem really was, "The island is short about two hundred doctors!" Hmm, with 8.5 percent unemployment nationwide, it seems there are job opportunities in Hawaii!

When the day of our dual appointments finally arrived and we had successfully navigated through the streets of Hilo, Pat pulled up in front of an obviously antiquated building in an area that looked like its neighbor buildings had already been condemned! I have to admit that my antennae shot up. *Who is this doctor anyway? Why is his office in such a dilapidated area? How good could he possibly be? Should we head for the hills while all body parts are still intact?* My mind was in a whirl. Pat seemed unfazed. As we climbed the steps, we entered into a whole new world…

A cool breeze met us at the threshold as we stepped into a huge waiting area with wall-to-wall paned windows. The receptionist window was on our immediate right, but our gaze beckoned us down a long, wide hallway sporting at least a dozen doors on both sides. The ceiling had to be twenty feet high, with walls painted in two conflicting shades of muted green. Pat leaned over and whispered in my ear, "An open-air concept." After a quick review of the extremely worn floor tile butting up to dark, stained hardwood leading down the corridor, I could have come up with another design evaluation that would neither be as creative or as forgiving! It just didn't look like any doctor's office I had ever visited. As we approached the receptionist's window, we were greeted by a very friendly young gal who looked to be in her early thirties. Directly behind her was a tall vase containing a display of Amaryllis blooms that looked like something out of a 1.800.FLOWERS commercial.

"Are those real?" I inquired.

"Oh, yes. A patient brought them in to us today," was her cheerful reply.

Are you kidding me? I thought. The antennae started to retract just a bit. We filled out the necessary paperwork while she took copies of our new Hawaii driver's licenses and insurance cards. Soon, an equally friendly nurse guided us through one of those dozen or more doors. While the nurse completed our basic medical charts, we pumped her with questions about the building. (Inquiring minds want to know.) She explained that it was originally a Japanese hospital built in 1936. (Okay, that explains the design concept!) Named after Dr. Zenko Motayoshi, who emigrated from Okinawa in 1924, the Motayoshi Hospital now houses two doctors offices. Our examination room was decorated with an antique medicine cabinet, still sporting the original two tiny (yet rusted) keys. Little carts on wheels, a folding privacy screen, ample magazines if one gets bored, and of course, the exam bed finished the decor. It turns out the exam room was originally the operating room!

Soon we met with Dr. Jung, a most agreeable man of Chinese descent. After spending a good half an hour discussing my medical history, he turned to focus on Pat. I slipped out of the room in search of an article Pat had mentioned about the building. After finding it framed and hanging on one of the muted green walls, I took it down and asked the sweet receptionist if she would make a copy for me. "Of course," was her reply. She handed me our driver's licenses, and then I scooted off to the ladies room. As I exited, I tucked the licenses under my arm. Please don't ask me why!

Soon, Pat was finished with his time with Dr. Jung, so I handed him his driver's license. Mine was already safely placed back in my wallet. He turned to me and asked, "Where is my medical card?" I replied that the receptionist hadn't returned it yet. Upon returning from the receptionist window, Pat said that she had given me the card along with our driver's licenses. Remembering that I had tucked them under my arm, I raised my right arm only to discover the card was still there! *Are you kidding me?* I had been walking around the office for ten minutes with his plastic medical card stuck under my armpit, and I didn't even know it was there! I laughed until the tears rolled down my face and onto that well-worn tile floor!

We skipped out the door toward our next task, praising God that the one and only doctor who would add us onto his patient list was the perfect doctor for us and housed in the most refreshing office we could possibly imagine!

What did I learn? How quick I am to jump to conclusions and make hasty evaluations based on practically no facts! I look at a building that, on the outside, seems to have no value, only to discover a rich history of service to the Japanese sugarcane workers and their families. I wonder why a doctor would accept us as new patients when twenty others said no, only to discover a committed family physician who takes the time to get to know his patients rather than rushing because we have a less-than-stellar insurance plan. And I am once again eternally grateful that God chooses to look at my heart rather than the human package that contains it. He has chosen me, in all my imperfections, to be adopted back into His flock, to walk with me daily through His Holy Spirit, and to eventually take up residence in heaven with Him. What more could I ask for? What more could we all ask for?

PS: I have also learned that just as socks can get lost in my dryer, a medical card can temporarily get lost under my arm!

{
God does not see as humans see. Humans look at outward appearances, but the Lord looks into the heart.

1 Samuel 16:7b, God's Word Translation
}

YURT FACTOID:

Pastoral nomads use two, or possibly three, Bactrian camels to carry a medium-sized yurt and household goods from encampment to encampment.

William Coperthwaithe

Waste Not
Want Not

Prior to making our move to Hawaii, I conducted extensive research as to how best to feed my horse and goats. The best source of information came in the form of a subscription to the award-winning *Malama-Lio Horse Journal* distributed throughout the Hawaiian Islands. The journal contained valuable guidance on all aspects of equine ownership. Each month, I devoured the articles and advertisements, pen and highlighter in hand, eventually developing relationships with various feed stores, farriers, as well as realtors who were horse owners. (I even became good buddies with the publisher, which led to a four-part story entitled "Journey to Paradise" featured in 2008, as well as a lead story entitled "Surviving a Coffin Bone Rotation," featured in their fall 2011 issue.) Within a short period, my plethora of notes found their way into a two-inch, three-ring binder, as I discovered just how different things are when you live on a rock in the middle of the Pacific Ocean. A comparison of hay is one excellent example.

In Big Bear, hay ran between twelve and eighteen dollars per bale depending upon the time of year and the type of hay purchased. If you hook up your trailer and haul it fifty miles to your buddy in Apple Valley, you might pay as low as eight dollars and twenty-five cents per bale. (During the decade we lived on the mountain, we used both methods.) But purchasing and receiving hay in Hawaii is a horse of a different color. Feed stores do not deliver it to your barn, and you pay a huge premium due to the transport required to move it from the mainland. Basically, the hay is shipped by barge, taking about two weeks from port to port. So by the time you picked it up, it is almost three weeks old. Hmm.

The next shocking reality is the price, thirty-four to forty-two dollars per bale, based again upon the type of hay and whom you purchase it from. Yikes! In addition, not all types of hay you either want or need is shipped to Hawaii. Alfalfa, Orchard, and Timothy are standard fair. (Smoke had been very happy and healthy eating Bermuda, not available in Hawaii!)

When we arrived on the island, I was prepared for serious sticker shock. I had done my homework and knew the investment that would be made monthly. At this point, you might be asking, "How much does one horse eat?" Good question. A bale of hay contains approximately twenty flakes. A horse usually eats two flakes per day. But for those who want to be exacting in quantity, the recommendation is to feed 1.5 to 2 percent of the horse's weight. So a one-thousand-pound equine will gobble up fifteen to twenty pounds daily. The bale usually weighs one hundred pounds, which equates to one bale lasting three and a half to five days.

Now, you may be asking yourself, "But can't a horse just graze on the pasture grass?" Another good question. Yes, they can. But horses require more than pasture grass to maintain good health. The grasses of Hawaii vary from area to area, even pasture to pasture, and can be deficient in certain minerals. (Did you know that out of the thirteen micro-climates in the world, Hawaii has eleven?) These grasses can also be very high in water content, often causing potbellies and sway-backs, not to mention other health issues.

While living in Big Bear, I would either pick up, or have delivered, twenty to thirty bales at a time. (I had a huge barn with one-fourth of the space designated for hay storage. And I didn't want to have to think about buying it every four weeks.) The new plan requires that we head to the feed store and purchase only six or seven bales, viewing it on the same scale as pure gold. Let's see—six bales times $38 equals $214 compared to $63 on the mainland! Ugh. That took a chunk out of my yard sale stash.

Keeping the hay dry, in a somewhat wet yet always moist environment, is paramount—for the budget, for the hay, and for the horse. Moldy hay has to be discarded—no ifs, ands, or equine butts about it.

We purchased a 5' × 7' Sunrise plastic storage shed to hold the precious commodity. This shed is a far cry from my 32' × 36' MD Barn. But what the heck. It works, and I am grateful. I look at every bale, every flake, every handful of hay as valuable. First, we drive one to two hours to pick it up. Then, I stack it in the shed. Then, it goes into the hay bag for Smoke's eating pleasure. Then, I rake up what has fallen to the ground, pitching it into the goat's area as feed and bedding. The painful part comes when I collect what isn't consumed and then spread it around trees and shrubs as composting material.

Smoke's eight to ten piles of manure, collected daily, also serves as a constant reminder that what goes in must come out, and at a very hefty price! Don't get me wrong here. I am very grateful that we live on twelve acres of rented pastureland. That alone saves us three hundred dollars per month on boarding fees. Smoke can graze during the day and then nibble from his hay bag throughout the night, cutting my hay bill right down the middle. Thank you, Jesus! And Smoke is able to live out his final season of life with his soft muzzle in the grassy rolling hills of the Hamakua Coast. What more can we both ask for?

{ The Lord is my shepherd, I shall not want. He makes me lie down in green pastures; He leads me beside quiet waters.
Psalm 23:1–2 }

YURT FACTOID:

The internal floor plan of a ger, Mongolian for yurt, is based on the four directions. The door always faces south, and the north is the place of sacred space. The western half of the ger is the men's side, and the eastern half is the women's area. The fire is in the sacred corner, and one moves around the yurt in a clockwise direction, following the path of the sun.

The Help

Ownership of animals is never a one-person job. The second you begin to plan a trip, whether overnight camping or a two-week whirlwind to the mainland, it becomes immediately obvious that help is required. When we moved to our little Paauilo paradise, I wondered how on earth we would find someone to care for our horse, two goats, and two felines. Honestly, we live two and a half miles off the main highway, and acres separate us from our nearest neighbors. Where would we find someone capable and willing to make the twice daily trek to our property? And what would it cost?

For the first two months, we had no need for help with our critters. But as a ten-day trip to California loomed in the not-so-distant future, I started to panic. Panic turned into prayer. And prayer turned into pursuit. I purposefully began to open my eyes to potential possibilities, inquiring with our neighbors as well as new friends who live in the area. Nothing surfaced.

One day, as I was driving down our one-lane country road, I stopped to say hi to Joe as he was motoring up. Joe and his wife, Kelly, live on the neighboring seven acres along with their three middle-aged kiddos, two cats, two dogs, and a steer named Stew. As is customary, we stopped, rolled down our side windows, and "talked story." Just before we waved good-bye, I casually mentioned our need for some help with our four-legged family members. "Would Taryn be interested?" I inquired. His oldest daughter is thirteen years old, loves animals, and "just might be interested," was his reply. Well, that is encouraging. Joe promised to talk it over with both Taryn and Kelly, getting back to me very soon.

A few days later, Taryn showed up at our appointed time, and her training began. First, I introduced her to Smoke and the two goats, noting important personality traits and safety precautions.

(There weren't many.) Then, I showed her where the hay and feed were stored, how to muck out the horse stall and refill with saw-dust shavings, clean the water buckets, the proper way to put the rain blanket and fly mask on and off Smoke, and the most important point of all: "Don't forget to lock the gates!" The last thing I wanted to hear was, "Smoke is running loose down Antone De Luz Road." (That precaution was ingrained in my mind while living fifty-five years in California and hearing the horror stories of loose horses hit and killed by cars!) I reminded her about the gates so many times I am sure she thought I resembled a broken record. (Or someone with an acute case of Alzheimer's.)

Then, with a small amount of trepidation, I handed her the upcoming schedule. *Here we go. Is she really ready to do this?* I thought to myself. Later, I called Kelly to confirm that she felt Taryn was up to the job. She said, "Yes. She is really looking forward to caring for your pets." Then, she added, "And we will help her initially." Whew. That was a huge relief. Parental guidance. I needed to hear that. I asked if seven dollars and fifty cents per visit was fair payment, and she agreed. We were in business.

When I was about nine or ten years old, I was hired to care for our neighbor's Nubian milking goats once or twice a year so they could take a family vacation. I thrived on the responsibility and the opportunity to earn my own money. I just loved sitting on the stool next to each goat, watching the milk squirt into the pail with each tender, yet firm, tug of the teats. Now as I trained and trusted Taryn, I felt a warm sense of passing the baton to a sweet young girl, help-ing her begin her own pursuit of independence, responsibility, and income. Could disaster strike? Possibly. Was help nearby? Definitely. Would it be worth the risk? I thought so.

We did a test run during an overnighter to the other side of the island. I must admit I was a bit nervous, calling a few hours after Taryn was scheduled to do her thing. I spoke with both Taryn and her mom, confirming that all went well. Mission accomplished! Her next assignment came sooner than later—an emergency trip to California immediately after my dad had his stroke. Pat would care for the animals each night, but Taryn would handle the morning responsibilities.

I am happy to report that she did a wonderful job. And with that, I knew God had heard and answered yet another prayer in a most remarkable way—care for our precious pets by a budding entrepreneur living only a few acres away…as the crow flies!

> Ask, and it will be given to you; seek, and you will find; knock, and it will be opened to you. For everyone who asks receives, and he who seeks finds, and to him who knocks it shall be opened.
>
> Matthew 7:7–8

YURT FACTOID:

Kirghiz yurts contain an explosion of color and pattern that includes intricately woven bands encircling the yurt inside and outside, patterned reed screens, brightly colored tassels hanging from the central ring, and colorful rugs covering the floor.

The Loofah

The Merriam-Webster Dictionary defines the loofah as "a sponge consisting of the fibrous skeleton of the fruit of a Loofah gourd." My definition is slightly different.

When we moved to our rented yurt, we left behind the handy-dandy washing machine and dryer. They didn't fit into our forty-foot shipping container. That was a huge disappointment for me but not a total loss. Our landlord had provided a slightly rusted washing machine, positioning it under the yurt lanai, directly next to the bathroom. It sported an outstanding ocean and rolling grass hills view. After four weeks of lugging our wet clothes to the P&J Laundromat, fifteen miles away, we decided to add a dryer...actually, an old-fashion clothesline. We had no money for materials, so in the spirit of Gilligan's Isle, we used thick bamboo poles scavenged from the road-side and bright-blue three-eighths-inch-diameter rope stretched from end to end. (I already had the wooden clothespins!) As our clothes flapped wildly in the trade winds, we marveled at this resurrected method of drying one's sheets, towels, undies, and assorted wearables.

But we soon discovered a scratchy snag in our laundry drying plan—towels dangling from a clothesline in the hot Hamakua sunshine dry stiff as surfboards! All sense of Downey softness is gone as the towels morph into huge rough rectangles of spun cotton. When I mentioned this fact to Pat, he simply stated that they were now loofahs, laughing all the way up the stairs and into the yurt. I stood there, staring at his backside, trying to find the truth in his matter-of-fact statement. Maybe a loofah towel isn't such a bad thing after all. Maybe scratching away the dead skin cells ultimately has its benefits. Then again, maybe fabric softener is the answer.

On my next trip to KTA, Hawaii's version of a grocery store, I invested in fabric softening crystals for the washer, wondering if I was overdoing it on the chemicals. Those crystals didn't work! So now I just loofah after every shower, content in knowing that as I scrub myself dry, I can say bye-bye to every dead skin cell I possess. Maybe I'm really on to something here.

> Then I will sprinkle clean water on you, and you will be clean; I will cleanse you from all your filthiness and from all your idols.
>
> Ezekiel 36:25

YURT FACTOID:

The Asian nomads place their furnishings against the wall, leaving the yurt's middle space open except for the central fire in colder seasons.

I Can't Hear You

Our Hakalau friend, John, often refers to our yurt as the "Conestoga wagon." This heavy, broad-wheeled-covered wagon was used extensively during the late eighteenth and nineteenth centuries as a method of migration southward through the Great Appalachian Valley. The only physical resemblance between our yurt and the Conestoga wagon is the vinyl cover that stretches across the top and down the side panels. But just as the Conestoga provided the ability to move personal possessions and cargo as early as 1717, the yurt, in its fundamental state, still provides nomadic tribes the ability to pack up and go based on weather and the needs of their grazing herds. Would we ever fold up our yurt and move it to another location? Nope! These twelve acres boast beautiful sunsets, lush tropical flora and fauna, and irreplaceable peace and quiet. Until the lights go out.

It never ceases to amaze me at the speed in which Pat falls asleep. Within a few short moments, his breathing slows down, the wiggling comes to a grinding halt, and a low rumble begins. That low rumble reminds me of the sound of a distant locomotive. But just as the choo-choo chugs closer and closer, the rumble from deep within my hubby grows in intensity. Soon that train is rumbling right through our yurt! How can he slumber in perfect peace with all that racket erupting from his throat?

During the first year of our marriage, I repetitively voiced my concerns over his snoring. In addition, his breathing ceased for what seemed like an eternity. (Secretly, I was afraid he had sleep apnea, a life-threatening disorder that causes extensive periods where the person is oxygen-deprived.) Finally, he agreed to make an appointment to see a sleep specialist. Poor guy! They put him through a battery of tests, including an overnight sleep evaluation. Why do they think a person can sleep on a narrow cot, sporting what appears to be an army-regulation blanket and sad excuse for a pillow, with the room temperature hovering slightly above freezing? When all was said and done, nothing was done. His problem became my problem. *Now what?*

As I considered my current challenge, noticing the bags under my own eyes, I remembered back to those girlie trips taken with good friend, Debi. She has the same sleep issue with her hubby, Skip. Debi's answer is simple—earplugs! So I invested in my own pair of the bright orange spongy model, crammed one in each ear, and… aah…blessed sleep. These little noise blockers are particularly helpful in the evening hours when Pat wants to watch TV and I want to read. I will turn down the bed covers, crawl in, reach for the ear sponges, and actually muffle out enough TV noise to concentrate. It isn't the perfect scenario, but it works when you live in a twenty-four-foot-diameter dwelling.

One day, shortly after moving into the yurt, Pat casually mentioned his need to purchase an "ear protection device." "What is that, and why would you need it?" I asked. He hemmed and hawed until I finally heard what he refused to say. I, too, was snoring! He kindly referred to it as a "gentle purr." Well, this caught me by surprise. "Oh, you mean you want headphones?" was my stunned reply. So after taking a few days to absorb this unpleasant fact, I suggested he try the ear sponges. He did, and they didn't…didn't block out enough "purring" for him to successfully stay asleep each night.

"Are you really going to wear headphones to bed?" I asked.

"Only when I need them!" he responded. Apparently, my snoring was an occasional irritation rather than the consistent train that roared through our yurt every night.

After a few false starts—ear protection devices that were either too uncomfortable or simply did not block out the "purr" as promised—he finally hit on the perfect model, the RYOBI Tek4, promoted as "noise suppression headphones." From a distance, they look like a headset worn by the pilot of a *Boeing 747*. Upon closer inspection, they strangely resemble a radio headset, complete with dials and knobs that allow the lucky wearer to customize the fit and the final function. Are you kidding me? Pat looks like he is in the sound studio of a radio station, absorbing the latest release by Yanni! Now if, and I mean *if,* I start to "purr," Pat straps on the Tek4. Most of the time, I don't know a thing about this little exercise. By morning's early light, my purring has miraculously subsided, and the noise suppression headphones find their way back to the top of the dresser!

Occasionally, Pat requires a mid-afternoon nap due to the two work-related back surgeries that keep him in a constant state of pain and often up between the wee hours of 1:00 and 5:00 a.m. Sleep deprivation just doesn't work for him. This mid-day nap thing can create quite a challenge if I am home. His eyes start to glass over, his speech slurs, and the poor guy heads for the Tek4 and bed. In addition, I often find him with a pillow over his head so as to usher in the darkness. Amazing but true, he quickly drops off to sleep. What is my confirmation? The train arrives right on schedule!

Honestly, I feel really bad about the Tek4 situation. I truly do. During this past year, I have done everything I can think of to reduce the amount of noise while Pat tries to sleep, whether he hits the rack at 8:30 p.m. after a rough day at the beach, at 7:00 a.m. when my internal alarm goes off and I am up and running, or anytime in between. Here are a few of my personal sacrifices:

- Eating chunky egg salad, painstakingly chopped with a knife and fork, rather than the super chopped up version created with my mini food processor.
- Turning my cell phone off or to the "silent" mode, then missing a very important call I have waited for all week.
- Stopping the ticktock of the West Germany brass and silver clock that hung in my dad's home for over forty years and now adorns one wall of our yurt.
- Going with store-bought orange juice rather than juicing oranges picked from our own trees.

- Tiptoeing throughout the yurt, with careful attention so as to keep from knocking over a protruding picture frame or stub my toe.

And here's the biggest sacrifice—moving my office outside the yurt and into our bathroom located under the lanai so I can make phone calls! (Please keep in mind that depending on the time of the year, we are two or three hours behind our friends and family in California and up to six hours behind contacts on the East Coast.) In an effort to provide Pat with those much-needed extra few hours of morning slumber, minus the chunky Tek4, I will grab my cell phone, notepad, pen, plus any necessary paperwork and head to the "downstairs office." To get the best phone connection requires that I stand at the bathroom window utilizing the four-inch ledge as my desk. This can be tricky as I often discover that I need a tidbit of information conveniently located up in the yurt. After asking if the party on the other end of the line would please wait a moment, I scoot up the lava rock pathway, tiptoe inside the yurt, grab what I need, and scurry back to the bathroom.

This is an exercise I have preformed a hundred times in the past months. If they only knew. And sometimes, if the wind is especially strong, I will hear them say, "Hello, I can't hear you!" Often, this problem can be rectified by moving the phone slightly to the left or right, and sometimes, we are simply disconnected. Such is the life of living off-grid with a five-foot satellite dish connecting you to the world… or not! And a hubby in deep slumber, snoring his brains out! Living in the round presents its own series of challenges—bringing the peace and quiet from outside in is just one of them. But as Pat and I creatively navigate through each challenge, we experience the joys of working together toward a common goal, placing each other's needs above our own. What a concept!

And, He said to him, "YOU SHALL LOVE THE LORD YOUR GOD, WITH ALL YOUR HEART, AND WITH ALL YOUR SOUL, AND WITH ALL YOUR MIND." This is the great and foremost commandment. The second is like it, "YOU SHALL LOVE YOUR NEIGHBOR AS YOURSELF."

Matthew 22:37–39

YURT FACTOID:

Students in Grass Valley, California, constructed the first complete yurt in North America in the early 1960s.

I'm Free!

Our yurt is located two and a half miles mauka from Highway 19, the island's best rendition of a freeway. Our country road was originally constructed of gravel, requiring four-wheel drive to navigate up and over the six gentle to steep slopes. Now asphalted, we as newcomers are able to easily ascend and descend in both the Chevy truck and my red Mini Cooper. There are approximately ten families living on our road. On any given day, various neighbors can be seen traveling up or down—by truck, by car, even on foot. This road offers an excellent, if not exhausting, exercise experience for all neighborhood inhabitants, including two frisky goats!

Once our goats, Gerdie and Heidi, adjusted to their paradise surroundings, I began to include them on my weekly walks. (Bottle-fed goat kids make excellent pets, closely bonding with their human family members.) Often, when we pop out of our gravel driveway on to this narrow, tree-lined road, we pass at least one of our neighbors. They always seem astounded that the goats not only come with me but stay near my side rather than bound off to greener pastures. These neighbors usually roll down their side windows to talk story, great for friendship building but terrible for maintaining my increased heart rate.

I remember the first time I took the girls for a walk. I called it our *maiden voyage*. At first, they were extremely tentative, staying close to me or wandering just a few feet away and then hip-hopping right back to my side. Soon Gerdie determined that the coast was clear, taking off at a crisscross canter ahead of me. Heidi quickly got the message, leaping straight into the air and then making a beeline toward her pasture pal. What a riot! Aside from the free entertainment, my eyes began to digest the beauty stretched out before me—no homes in sight—only rolling grass hills, magnificent Eucalyptus and Ohia trees, grazing cattle with nursing calves, and the azure blue Pacific Ocean dead ahead. The air was crystal clear, offering up fragrant whiffs from nearby ginger plants. *Aah...this is heaven on earth*, I thought to myself.

Observing the obvious freedom the goats were enjoying directed my thoughts toward the freedom I too was enjoying. I realized I was finally free from all the emotional, physical, and financial concerns surrounding our oceanic move. Concerns like: Would the horse and goat survive the nineteen-hour travel? Would we survive the move? Would we be accepted? Would I adjust from living in a three-thousand-square-foot home to a 450 not-so-square-foot yurt? Would our family and friends ever come to visit? Could I find work? Would we ever get out of debt?

At the close of this little burden-baring inventory, I took a deep breath, offering up a prayer of thanks that many of these concerns had already been taken care of. Then, I kicked up my heels, jogging to catch up with the girls. All three of us were free—finally free. And it felt so good!

Prior to our move, a few family members and well-meaning friends asked us if we were running away rather than facing the giants in our lives. Pat and I discussed this many times and were both in agreement that, through prayer and Godly wisdom, we had faced those giants. When the e-mail came, inviting us to house-sit the ranch of friends on the Big Island, we felt it was God's open door toward a better way of life. He provided a new, less traveled path. It was our responsibility to take those first tentative steps. Once the wheels of change were in motion, everything began to fall into place. We were offered our realtor's yurt for as long as we needed it. The savings we enjoyed through renting and living off-grid enabled us to continue to slowly pay off our enormous debt of over $600,000. I found part-time employment as an assistant to a property manager, helping her clean houses. (That was a humbling experience compared to my six and a half years as the buyer/operations manager for eight gift stores for the San Bernardino National Forest Association!) And our family and friends began to schedule their Hawaii vacations!

As Gerdie, Heidi, and I huffed and puffed toward home, my mind took me back almost four and a half years to a prophetic moment I will never forget. It was the Fifth Annual Christian Women's Gathering, an inter-denominational event I co-founded and co-coordinated with my dear friend, Belinda. Our theme was "Pathway to God's Presence: In Every Season of Life." The day had offered up a roller coaster of emotions. Pat and I had put our home on the market a few weeks earlier, and we were confident our time in Big Bear was drawing to a close.

The Christian Women's Gathering held a very special place in my heart, and I was having a difficult time letting it go. Each year, coordination for the Gathering required the creative input and exhaustive efforts of at least a dozen prayerful women, and sometimes a few supportive husbands. Although Teresa and Vern were in the midst of moving to the quaint town of Forks, Washington, Vern kept his promise to donate a painting for our fundraising efforts. They were almost packed when Teresa called to tell me the painting was complete, and I should come pick it up before one of her toddlers used it as a finger painting board. I drove right over in great anticipation.

Our theme the prior year was "On Wings Like Eagles: An Appointment with the Trinity!" Vern had graciously sculpted from wood, an enormous eagle with outstretched wings, now proudly displayed in the foyer of a local home for elderly Big Bear residents. I couldn't wait to see what God had inspired him to paint this year. After parking the car and locating Teresa in her partially emptied living room, I followed her to the garage. As soon as my eyes focused on it, I gasped and said, "That's me!" My connection to the painting was instantaneous. A young girl stood at a crossroads: to the left was lush tropical trees, shrubs, and blue water; to the right was dry, unfertile soil, a virtual wasteland stretched out under the hot glare of a cloudless summer sky. The flowing ribbons of her bonnet and simple sway of her ankle-length skirt hinted of a gentle breeze. I couldn't see her face, but I knew it was me. I realized that the decisions I would make in the future would take me down one of these two paths. Would I make the right decisions, leading me to abundance or take a mis-step and head, unknowingly, toward desolation?

I carefully transported the treasured artwork home, astounded at God's handiwork through Vern. For the next three days, I often found myself in my home-based office, just sitting and staring at that young girl. I knew the painting would be raffled off. And I knew at that point, I would have to let it go. I never ever included myself in the raffle drawings. It just didn't feel like the right thing to do.

By the time the raffle rolled around, the air felt electrified as women anticipated the drawing for Vern's painting. I stood at the podium, microphone in one hand, holding the overflowing basket of raffle tickets in the other. Teresa stepped forward to draw the final ticket for the painting, my painting. Earlier in the day, after announcing our list of donated gifts, I shared my immediate connection to the young girl and the journey she was about to make. I asked the ladies if I could put just one ticket into the raffle basket. (In my heart, I had already prepared to willingly let it go to someone else.) Throughout the day, I heard confirmations that I should not only put one ticket in, but many tickets, that precious women were actually buying tickets for me, that at least one woman had felt led to give me the painting if she won it! I was speechless at the love these daughters of our King poured out to me.

Teresa selected the winning ticket. Then, she handed it to me so I could announce the numbers. I slowly read each one. No response. I repeated them again. Dead silence permeated the huge meeting room. I repeated them a third time, and someone finally shouted, "I think that is Linda's ticket, and she left fifteen minutes ago."

With no way to confirm this, and the pre-announced decision that "The winner must be present to win," Teresa drew a new ticket. As I read off the numbers, my eyes glanced down to the ticket resting on the podium, a duplicate of the only one I had placed in the basket. Each number I called off matched my ticket! I stood there, before over one hundred women, in complete shock! When I shouted that the numbers matched my ticket, pandemonium broke out. Tears began to fall from my eyes, and for once, and I mean once in my life, I was speechless!

God, in His infinite love for me, guided the paintbrush held by Vern and then supernaturally placed that prophetic vision into my trembling hands, a visual confirmation of the journey, the path He was planning for me. Did I have the courage to take the required steps of faith? That painting hung directly across from my office desk for another three and a half years, providing immeasurable strength and encouragement during a time wrought with frustration, confusion, and, ultimately, faith in the One who had given me a tiny glimpse into my not-too-distant future.

Now, as the goats and I rounded the last bend toward the yurt, I once again cherished in my heart that amazing moment in time, thanking my heavenly Father for His love and His provision. I was free, free indeed!

P.S: By the time I picked up the painting, Vern had already left for Washington. Teresa and their three kiddos would follow directly after the close of the Christian Women's Gathering. Two weeks after the Gathering, I was finally able to call Vern to thank him for his creative and generous gift and to share the supernatural story of how I had received it. Vern, with no encouragement from me, announced that the hint of blue water at the end of the lush pathway was, in fact, the ocean, not a lake.

"I know, Vern. I know!"

> Therefore, if the Son shall make you free, you shall be free indeed.
>
> John 8:36

YURT FACTOID:

Today, we not only have the womblike indigenous Central Asian yurts, the Turkic üy, and the Mongolian ger, but also three modern versions: the Tapered Wall yurt, the Modern Fabric yurt, and the Frame Panel yurt.

Gerdie and Heidi
(From top to bottom)

Motayoshi Hospital Built in 1936

My Fearless Farrier, Susanella, and Smoke

Smoke's 30th Birthday

Our Yurt Bathroom

Jen, Heidi and Gerdie on a walk

"Pathway"
By Vern Hestand

Season Two

February–April
2012

The Property Manager

One of the more difficult moments I experienced, prior to leaving Big Bear, was handing in my letter of resignation. For six and a half years, I had held the position of buyer/operations manager for the San Bernardino National Forest Association, overseeing eight gift stores on the Angeles and San Bernardino National Forests. I loved my job, especially displaying the nature-related merchandise I carefully selected, while attempting to meet the challenges associated with keeping the stores afloat in the midst of a turbulent recession. I will never forget the lavish bon voyage party Sarah, the executive director, gave me. Held at a local resort, it was attended by staff, friends, family, as well as both in-town and out-of-state consignment vendors. My heart was touched by the beautiful and thoughtful gifts they presented to me, expressing the depth of our long-standing relationships.

I shed many tears as we sat around the extended tables, sharing stories and saying our good-byes. One question repetitively came up prior to our move. "How will you get a job?" We were moving to the rural community of Paauilo, and with the recession in full swing, opportunities for employment would be few and far between. I have always been of the mind that if you want to work, you will find work. It may not be a job you did in the past. And you may not make the same wage. But attitude counts. Plus, I had 100 percent faith that because God had opened the yurt door for us to move to this area, it was ultimately His responsibility to provide me with employment. My job was to keep my eyes, ears, and heart open to His leading.

My hubby is about as friendly as they come, always waving to our neighbors as we pass each other on our rural road, often pulling over to talk story. We both feel that it is very important to not only meet our neighbors but also develop friendships whereby they can count on us and vice versa. Dianna is a close neighbor living just over the hill. One day, while we were chatting through the driver's side windows of our matching siren-red Mini Coopers, I invited her to the yurt. She knew Bailey, our realtor and landlord, and I think she was just a bit curious as to how we were living in this 450 not-so-square-foot space. Shortly after crossing the threshold and receiving a glass of sun tea, she complimented me on my interior design efforts. I explained that we had moved from a three-thousand-square-foot home, and after four yard sales, furniture sent to consignment stores and given to family and friends, this, in addition to what was stored in a twenty-foot shipping container, was what "made the cut." I inquired as to her line of work. She shared that she was a property manager.

"What exactly does a property manager do?" I asked. She explained that she manages numerous rental properties for owners who live off-island: checking guests in and out, taking care of any problems (and here's the important part), cleaning each home or condo when the guests leave. As she chatted away, my mind was in a whirl. *I can help her. I can clean homes, no problem*! I finally asked if she needed any help. She said she would call me the next time she had a "turn-around." (Later, I discovered that a turn-around happens when one set of guests leave and another comes in within four short hours.) *That went well*, I thought as we gave each other a quick hug and she exited for home. A few weeks later, Dianna called to see if I was available to help her clean a very large home on the Kona Coast. Two days later, she picked me up in her Mini, and off we motored. I have to say that cleaning someone else's luxuriously appointed home, while I was enjoying my time in the yurt, was a humbling experience, as well as a completely new line of work.

A verse in the Bible kept running through my mind and heart: "Do everything as for the Lord." I knew He had provided this job. I also knew that I wanted to do the very best I could, for Him and for Dianna. As I learned her cleaning techniques, I was able to contemplate my current situation. I was living in a twenty-four-foot-diameter space, with a small bathroom located outside the yurt and under the attached lanai. My beautiful home on the mainland sat vacant, now valued at less than half of what it was worth five years ago. Scrubbing toilets, polishing Koa wood furniture, and hosing off lanais provided me with time to pray, to ask God to give me a thankful heart, and to increase my trust in Him. He did just that every time Dianna and I worked side-by-side.

Two unexpected things occurred during my house-cleaning experiences: (1) I became very good friends with Dianna. Not only do we both share an obsession with owning siren-red Mini Coopers, we insist on wearing our hair very long, and skipping most of the makeup. Her home is truly one of a kind, nestled against a forest background, with sweeping pasture and ocean views. She loves antiques as much as I do, with a vintage wood-burning stove and enormous cast iron sink in her kitchen. (2) I actually earn more per hour cleaning houses than I did at my previous job with the National Forest Association! So much for thirty-five years of retail experience, an international award for special events, and my extensive people skills. (Non-profits just can't keep up with the going rate, but the rewards are endless.)

Here's the truth. God is in charge of every facet of our lives if we give Him the steering wheel. As Creator of the universe, He is more than able to intersect our lives with the lives of others, which, if we are open-minded, provide answers to our immediate needs, and in most creative and unexpected ways. The money I earn often pays for our groceries and gas. This job gives us just what we need, and at the exact moment we need it. How grateful I am.

{ Whatever you do, do your work heartily, as for the Lord rather than for men; knowing that from the Lord you will receive the reward of the inheritance. It is the Lord Christ whom you serve.

Colossians 3:23–24 }

YURT FACTOID:

Dickenson's Reach, named for poet Emily Dickenson, is tucked away on the rocky coastal shoreline of Northern Maine. This one-of-a-kind retreat is the home of William Coperthwaite, designer of the Tapered Wall yurt, and founder and director of the Yurt Foundation.

Baby, Oh Baby

I am an animal lover—by nature and by rearing. At three years of age, my mom gave me a gorgeous calico kitten. Of course, we named her Callie. A few years later, Callie proudly presented us with a litter of three adorable kittens. We kept the tiny orange tabby and named him Pooh. By the time I completed the summer of my ninth year, I had painstakingly earned fifty dollars by baking and selling cookies door-to-door while peddling my bike up and down the hills of our rural neighborhood. (It was actually safe to do that forty-six years ago!) My parents matched my profits, and Folly, a twenty-six-year old nag, I mean mare, miraculously arrived on our property. This good-natured equine allowed a green equestrian to creep all over her, practice newly acquired grooming skills sanctioned by our local 4-H Club, and ride her along the same cookie business route.

Later, two show horses and one Nubian goat were added to the eclectic mix, along with two Bassett hounds—Beau and Boomerang. (Throckmorten, another lumbering Bassett, lived down the road. Can you imagine naming a dog Throckmorten?) Somewhere between nine and sixteen years of age, we cared for an opossum named Ophelia, who had fallen into our pool, three rabbits that multiplied at a frightening pace, plus a variety of birds and reptiles. It was great! (I don't think my dad would agree.)

After moving to the yurt, Pat and I were of the same mind to reproduce the little flock of chickens we had enjoyed while living in Big Bear. (No, those chickens were long gone prior to our move to Hawaii.) Chickens are cheap entertainment, and the eggs are considered a financial and healthful bonus.

One day, as I was heading toward the yurt after a quick ride on Smoke, my eyes caught movement on the gravel path up ahead. As I focused, I saw that it was a tiny chick scrambling to and fro. *Wow!*

We can start our flock for free with this little one! With a bit of effort, I was able to carefully capture the creature in my hands. Just as I was beginning to inspect her, my peripheral vision caught another motion to the left, as simultaneously, my ears heard the wild flapping of wings—large wings—and an unusual squawking sound that registered "danger" throughout my entire body. I quickly looked over my shoulder only to find an enormous wild turkey flying at me like Tom Cruise in his *Top Gun* fighter jet! Holy you-know-what!

No time to think. I gently threw the fledgling into a patch of nearby grass and ran for my life! Thankfully, Momma was only interested in ushering her one lost peeper back into the fold and I was happy to let her do just that! Whew…that was a close call!

On a side note, multi-award-winning singer-songwriter, Paul Overstreet, wrote a catchy and truthful tune entitled, "If Momma Ain't Happy, Nobody's Happy!" That turkey momma was going to get her chick back, or else. This momma was more than happy to oblige!

> What man among you, if he has a hundred sheep and has lost one of them, does not leave the ninety-nine in the open pasture and go after the one which is lost until he finds it?
>
> Luke 15:4

YURT FACTOID:

"Circular living provides a balance of looking inward and outward, looking out at the natural environment and surroundings but then coming in again to self and the hearth."
David Raitt, yurt builder

The Gift

I hold many desires deep within my heart. Some desires are big, and I share them with others. Some might appear to be small, less important, and possibly only mentioned in such a way as to be easily passed over. On one recent, and seemingly uneventful, Sunday morning, God chose to fulfill one of my small, unspoken desires.

I was standing in the breezeway after church, nibbling on snacks, when I was approached by a friend. "A kitten showed up at our house, and we wondered if you might want to adopt it?" This got my attention. Rich explained that the kitten was about two months old, very loving, and...an orange tabby! (I adore orange tabbies, as evidenced by those I have loved and cared for in previous years, actually decades: Keaton, Stanley, Beeswax, Stuart, and Stanley Number Two.) I had secretly grumbled that the last two cats I had acquired (of which I still own) were "lackluster kitties." One is gray, and one is black. Yikes, why not an orange tabby? I told Rich that I would think about this...

As each day passed, I became more excited about this little guy. Anticipation built, and by Tuesday night, I had decided he was to be mine. I even named him Tucker, thinking we could just tuck him somewhere on the property. (No, Pat knew nothing of all that was going through my pea brain! Poor guy.) By Wednesday morning, I had made arrangements to pick Tucker up later in the day after running errands in Waimea. The pick-up location became the local vet's office so he could be rid of the nasty worms and ear mites young kittens usually possess. After a full day with the Kona Women's Connection, I swung by to collect my little package, sight yet unseen! They brought him out in a purple kitty carrier. As I peeked inside, there he was, the perfect little guy complete with serious orange stripes and polka dots body-wide, white paws, and a twinkle in his eyes! He was in great shape. Then, the most amazing (at least for me) thing occurred.

The vet casually mentioned that "he" was actually a "she." After challenging him, noting how rare female orange tabbies are, the vet proceeded to carefully remove the kitty from the carrier and then lift its tail for my inspection. At that precise moment, I knew I had just received a gift from my heavenly Father! In my fifty-five years of being owned by felines, I had only seen one orange tabby of the female variety. I had secretly wanted one, but I never dreamed that I would ever have one. They are so very rare! As we drove home, Tucker immediately morphed into Makai and sat happily in her purple (the color for royalty, by the way) kitty carrier. It was hard for me to keep my eyes on the road. I just couldn't stop staring at her. And I think I was still in a bit of shock!

So what does all this boil down to? God knows the secret desires of our hearts! When we are in relationship with Him, through His beloved Son, Jesus Christ, the floodgates remain open to receive His blessings and at just the right moment. What do you secretly hope for? He knows. Whether you take it to Him in prayer, verbalize it to others, or just hold on tight in silence, be prepared! And when the surprise arrives, let's always remember who and where it came from, giving Him praise from a thankful heart!

> Every good thing bestowed and every perfect gift is from above, coming down from the Father of lights, with whom there is no variation or shifting shadow.
>
> James 1:17

YURT FACTOID:

One of the tangible advantages of yurts is that there are no corners to catch the wind, which naturally flows over and around the yurt.

The Promise

One of the most important conversations Pat and I had prior to moving to the Big Island centered on how we would handle things if someone in our family suddenly became ill. We made a promise to one another that if a family member on the mainland needed us, we would go, no questions asked, regardless of the cost. On April 13, we put that promise to the test...

The eve of April 12 produced a series of phone calls from my brother, Jeff, culminating in the announcement that our dad had suffered a stroke early that morning, had laid on his bathroom floor, wrapped around the toilet for twelve hours, and was now on his way to Hoag Memorial Hospital in Newport Beach, California.

Needless to say, I was stunned! Just three and a half months earlier, I had enacted, in Dad's living room, a scene whereby he suffers a stroke or heart attack and falls to the floor, unable to reach the phone to call for help. I wanted him to wear one of those med-alert necklaces or bracelets. Pretty basic considering he lives alone and was just shy of his eighty-seventh birthday. Amidst peals of laughter from my siblings and Dad, his answer was, "No. I don't need that!" Well, he did eventually need that.

Pat and I live in a twenty-four-foot-diameter yurt, with rooms separated simply by the different types of furniture you find in specific rooms of a home. The bathroom is conveniently located outside, down a lava rock pathway, and under the yurt. Since Pat usually sleeps until 8:30 or 9:00 a.m. due to back issues that rob him of sleep between the wee hours of 3:00 and 7:00 a.m., any early morning phone calls have to be made from the bathroom so as not to disturb him. At 5:00 a.m. on April 13, I made my way down to the bathroom, cell phone in hand, to try to speak with Dad. Miraculously, my brother was able to hold the phone to Dad's drooping mouth, and when I heard his garbled speech, I burst into uncontrollable sobs. I felt so helpless 2,506 miles away. As the oldest of three children, I felt it was my responsibility to be there.

After a brief time with Dad, my brother got back on the line. He informed me that the hospital was conducting a myriad of tests, pumping Dad with fluids for dehydration and infection, and binding up a dozen skin tears he had received while trying to drag himself from the bathroom to a phone. (Dad always refers to his skin as "corrugated cardboard." But in reality, it is closer to corrugated tissue paper!) When I finally said good-bye to my brother, I mopped up my tears, marched back up to the yurt, woke Pat from a deep sleep, and announced, "I have to get on the next flight to Orange County!" He quickly agreed. At 9:05 p.m., as I began the five-and-a-half-hour flight to California, I quietly murmured the one thousandth prayer to my heavenly Father. Then, I allowed myself to consider the various paths set before me. Would I make it in time to see Dad? If he survived, would there be long term irreversible physical limitations? Could he eventually return to his own home and life as he knew it? What about insurance coverage, handling his estate, Pudge, the fat feline who gave him such joy? My head was spinning, but it just about spun off when I finally made it to the hospital seven hours later.

As I found my way to Dad's hospital room, two pairs of bloodshot eyes met mine at his door. My sister, Debbie, and Jeff had been holding a bedside vigil throughout night. One look at Dad was enough for me to realize that although he had been a marine in World War II, and the recipient of the Purple Heart after surviving a sniper bullet that ripped through his left arm and chest, he was in for the fight of his life now. As my siblings and I stood by his bed, we committed to join him in this fight!

Dad is probably no different from you or me. He has always felt in control of his life, determining where he would live, the job he would take, the car he would drive, the dinner he would enjoy. In a blink of an eye, it all changed. And it can happen to anyone at anytime.

I have learned so much through our attempt to sell our home, the move to a rented yurt in Hawaii, and now, Dad's stroke. I have learned that I, too, am not really in control. None of us are! I couldn't control much of what has happened to us over the past four years as we tried to sell our home for a fair price and retire in Hawaii. And I sure couldn't keep Dad from suffering the trauma of April 12. So if we aren't in control, who is? I choose to believe, and feel confident in my heart, that what the Bible says is true. God is the One who gives us the precious gift of life. Only He knows how many days we have on this earth. He knows the beginning from the end. And although He is not the one who causes the trials of our lives, He is there to pick us up, dust us off, and place us on a new path. Peace for whatever trials we face comes through being in a personal relationship with Him, through His Son, Jesus Christ, the peace that surpasses all human understanding. I asked for that peace over twenty-six years ago, and He has never failed me. If you find that you need peace, just ask Him for it. But first, you'll need to ask Him to come into your heart, to forgive you of all the nasty stuff in your life, and to give you a new life with Him, both here on earth and for all eternity in heaven.

> Peace I leave with you; My peace I give you; not as the world gives, do I give to you. Let not your heart be troubled, nor let it be fearful.
>
> John 14:27

YURT FACTOID:

People seem to sleep better in yurts, and they often dream more.

Dad

There are pluses and minuses to being born an A-type personality. I know because I am one! A-types take control of situations. We tend to be the administrators, the go-to people for something as simple as a family get-together or as complicated as maneuvering through a family crisis. The challenge comes in balancing our seemingly inexhaustible energy and ability to make decisions on the fly, with the invaluable need to respect, listen to, and include input from others. When I drug myself through the front doors of Hoag Hospital, after exiting a red-eye flight from the Big Island to LAX, I wasn't sure what I would find. Would Dad still be with us? Would he remember me? What was the extent of his injuries after suffering a stroke forty-eight hours earlier? And where would we go from here?

As I tiptoed into the sterile room that held my precious father, my eyes landed upon a man who had obviously suffered. His bandaged "corrugated tissue paper" skin tears and multiple bruises spoke of his unsuccessful struggle to crawl out of his bathroom, get to a phone, and call for help. The IV methodically dripped fluids containing medications through his veins and into his struggling organs, while a monitor peeped and blipped, noting Dad's vitals. But it was the foggy eyes that told the real story. Dad had suffered a vascular stroke. In his case, it affected the right side of his brain, causing visual damage to the left side of his face, which now drooped. His speech was garbled, and he couldn't swallow correctly. Miraculously, he had no paralysis, and it appeared that his long-term memory was fully intact. Those were the blessings!

Over the next seven days, this A-type flew into high gear. Initially, I had to pay attention to every word that came out of the seemingly endless stream of doctors and nurses filing in and out of his room, noting terms and conditions I was not familiar with. "Who was in charge of what?" became a constant question I asked. In the middle of trying to understand Dad's current condition, I had to make decisions regarding immediate treatments, provide requested paperwork for the hospital, help decide where he would go when he left the hospital, all in the midst of staying as calm as a cucumber whenever I was in Dad's presence.

Then there was the all-important meeting with Dad's estate planner, his credit union, ordering new checks, getting paperwork notarized, digging through a ton of his financial files, making plans for his feline, packing up the valuables we didn't feel comfortable keeping in his now empty duplex, calls to Medicare and his secondary insurance company, plus a myriad of seemingly endless details, all while communicating and sometimes meeting multiple times daily with my brother and sister. I felt like I had entered the twilight zone!

After about four days at Hoag Hospital, and the insertion of a feeding tube into his stomach, we were told that Dad could be moved to a nearby rehabilitation facility. Jeff and I visited a number of suggested facilities and then made the decision to have him admitted to Crystal Cove Care Center in Newport Beach. After packing up the recommended clothing and personal items Dad would require, I drove to Crystal Cove and waited for the ambulance delivering my precious cargo. We were entering a new, and hopefully brief, season of life.

A few days after getting Dad settled into his new room and a fairly rigorous routine of speech, occupational, and physical therapy, I had to leave him in the capable care of my siblings and board a plane back to Hawaii. I didn't want to go. I didn't want to leave him, but I had to return home so that Pat could board a plane to California thirty-six hours later to visit our newly born first grandchild. It was my turn to hold down the fort...I mean the yurt.

As I sat in my assigned seat on the *Boeing 757*, I reflected on the hundreds of decisions I had already made on behalf of Dad, decisions that gratefully were made with the help and input of my brother and sister. We were singular in our thinking, "What is best for Dad?" There were no arguments, no hurt feelings, only three nervous adult kids working together. I was scheduled to return ten days later, staying for two weeks this time. What would happen in the interim? What would need to be done upon my return? Only heaven knew for sure.

I don't think it really matters what type of personality you are. When life throws you a curve ball, it can turn your world upside down. Other people can help to a degree. Then, it's just you and your situation, right? I don't believe so. When I was in the midst of a bad marriage, I cast my cares upon the Lord. When I was going through a divorce, I cast my cares upon the Lord. When I purchased my very own home, I cast my cares upon the Lord. When I had a wayward son, I...you got it...I cast my cares upon the Lord. Now, as Dad's life hangs in the balance, I automatically cast my cares upon the One who has been faithful to me for the past twenty-six years. When I am scared, He gives me comfort. When I am confused, He gives me wisdom. And when I am hopeless, He gives me hope! What more can I ask for?

{
...casting all your anxiety upon Him because He cares for you.

1 Peter 5:7
}

YURT FACTOID:

"Imagine what would happen if three hundred million people were concerned with building a better world! This would be a social revolution such as has never been conceived. The key difference would be people coming together to the realization that it is their world: that it can be changed, that they can, should, and must have a role in redesigning that world."
Bill Coperthwaite

Look Up!

There are many elements to yurt living that make it both unique and enjoyable. The ceiling is just one of them. Our little love yurt offers only one entrance/exit. We refer to it as the front door. Upon entering, one almost instinctively looks up as the eye follows forty-two 2" × 4" rafters attached to a center ring. The crowning jewel is a six-foot pop-open acrylic dome creating additional light and ventilation inside, as well as a peekaboo to the outside world. I believe that one of the key factors to successful small-space living is a high ceiling. Ours is approximately fifteen feet from top to bottom. This design concept not only enables our lightweight structure to stand on its own, with no interior beams or load-bearing walls, but also creates a sense of roominess throughout the 450 not-so-square feet.

My favorite view from inside is looking out, more specifically up, especially while dropping off to sleep each night. The combination of circular bone-colored vinyl and naturally-stained wooden rafters create a vision similar to that of the sun's rays shooting 360 degrees from its center, or petals exiting the seed-filled center of an enormous sunflower. On a clear night I can see a myriad of stars suspended from the evening sky. If sleep escapes me I attempt to count those stars, far better than drumming up a vision of sheep and then unsuccessfully trying to count them as they scramble around in my head.

Occasionally, after giving Pat his good night smooch and pulling the covers up to my chin, I lie on my back, look up, and behold a stunning view—the moon, whether sliver or full, depending on the time of year. I lay there mesmerized, thinking that every home should include a dome! (I guess skylights could be considered the next best thing, but not as large or attractive, in my humble opinion.)

One of the reasons we chose to move to the Hamakua Coast, and more specifically, the small town of Paauilo, was the weather. Over a four-year period, Pat had conducted extensive research throughout the island to determine what climate and area would work best for our needs. The following parameters were kept at the forefront of our minds: sun, rainfall, trade winds but no gale force winds, average temperatures, and, by the way, no pig or rooster farms. Hands down, Paauilo was it! In addition to considering how best to sustain our animals—lush pastureland was the ticket—we also wanted a comfortable living environment for ourselves. This would ultimately include a combination of dew suspending from blades of grass in the early morning hours, to drizzle from passing clouds, to the occasional downpour that could last anywhere from an hour to three days. Over time, I came to view these forms of H_2O as life-sustaining, marveling at the fact that if we captured the water properly, we didn't have to pay for it. What a concept!

The very first thing I do upon waking up every morning is look up. The dome tells me what my ears might not have heard through the night. *Did it rain?* If I see circular coin-size drops on the dome, I know the pasture has been nourished and the water tanks replenished.

One early morning, while sitting at my end of the couch with pen and notepad in hand, I looked up to see if the drops were there. What did I discover? Instead of finding the telltale remnants of a passing wee hours rain cloud, my eyes focused on light-blue sky, a few twinkling stars, and a half moon staring back at me. (It always seems a bit of an oxymoron to see the moon during daylight, especially through the ceiling of your home.)

How totally cool…a sunny morning. The perfect morning to climb onto Smoke's back and ride the hills of Paauilo. And that's exactly what we did.

Living in our nomad-inspired yurt offers not only a view to what the evening has provided, and the day's weather to come, but also a sense of comfort. I am constantly reminded of the heavenly home that will someday be mine, the family members that paved the way, and my heavenly Father's constant watch over me as well as those I love. The universe is an unfathomable expanse of space that can make you and I seem microscopic by comparison. And it's true. We are microscopic. Yet God sees us clearly, the trials we face, as well as the joy of our successes. He sees us and He hears us. No dome required... just a relationship with Him through His Son, Jesus Christ. How simple. How profound.

> O Lord, our Lord, how majestic is Your name in all the earth, who have displayed Your splendor above the heavens! From the mouth of infants and nursing babes You have established strength because of Your adversaries, to make the enemy and the revengeful cease. When I consider Your heavens, the work of Your fingers, the moon and the stars, which You have ordained; what is man that You take thought of him, and the son of man that You care for him? Yet You have made him a little lower than God, and You crown him with glory and majesty! You make him to rule over the works of Your hands; You have put all things under his feet, all sheep and oxen, and also the beasts of the field, the birds of the heavens and the fish of the sea, whatever passes through the paths of the seas. O Lord, our Lord, how majestic is Your name in all the earth!
>
> Psalm 8:1–9

YURT FACTOID:

Yurt fabrics are available in a multitude of fireproof, waterproof, and mildew resistant material and coating options. Colors range from beige to forest green to terracotta red and even indigo blue.

Comfort in Communication

I had just experienced one of those days where I couldn't make an ounce of headway. My fingers were in so many pies, and try as I might, I felt like I was taking one step forward and two steps back. Finally, I told Pat, "I need to go outside and spend some time with Smoke." He agreed. I mucked out the stall and put in fresh shavings, scrubbed out the two water barrels refilling them with fresh water, stuffed ten empty feed bags with hay for future feedings, and pushed the wheel barrel around the pasture picking up a dozen piles of poop.

Then, I captured the Palomino, groomed him, got his gear on, and headed out the back forty for a much-needed ride. Whew...I was already feeling better! Our neighbor, he goes by Bully, has staked his cows all over the hills of Paauilo—including those viewed from our lanai. Smoke does not like the cows! During our afternoon trek, we passed three of those staked cows. On the return trip, the bovines decided to talk with one another, great "bellows" ringing throughout our peaceful rolling hills. *What on earth are they saying? Do they find comfort in communicating even though they can't see each other?* I wondered.

When we got back home, I felt like I needed more riding time, so we took a turn up our gravel driveway. Although I couldn't see them, I could hear conversation coming from a flock of wild turkeys that often congregate at the top of our street. Smoke heard them too! In an effort to avoid potential disaster, we cut through the front pasture, only to discover a hidden path. Off we went, winding down another tree-lined driveway that led us across a gulch and into the back pasture. But not before we flushed out four members of that turkey tribe who were on a journey of their own!

Boy, did they have a lot to say—either to one another or to us. How could I tell? I do know they were females because they did not strut their stuff with fanned tails, like the males of the flock. What on earth were they saying to one another? Based on the intensity of their communication, it must have been very important! This diatribe of conversation between God's creatures reminded me of a group of ladies seated around a table at their favorite restaurant.

God created women to communicate, twenty-five thousand words per day, I am told. This constant cackle is *not* our fault; it's in our DNA to communicate! Amidst all the commotion, I began to reflect on the dear friends I have been blessed with over the years, friends both near and far. I remembered hearing the promise that no matter where I went, God would always provide Christian friends. Now I can see that promise fulfilled in the gift of friendship I have received since moving here. There is Sandy, with her quiet demeanor, yet witty writing prose; Gloria, a rekindled friendship from high school; the ladies in my Bible Study; and Lisa, my ebullient boss and chairperson of the Kona Women's Connection. At any given time, I can pick up the phone or snag one of these gals by the arm to begin our own diatribe on activities, challenges, hopes, fears, needs, or joy. I can pour my heart out to any one of these precious girlfriends. And when I stop to take a breath, they will jump in to offer me words of wisdom, support, encouragement, even laughter, and a good old hug. Then, they reciprocate with situations in their own lives. And around and around we go!

But what happens when we are alone or, at least, feel alone? Who is there to lead us by the hand, carry us to safety, lend an ear, and whisper words of comfort to our heart and soul? The Bible tells me that Jesus will draw near to me when I draw near to Him. Whether I am riding Smoke through the hills of Paauilo, sitting on my couch in our cozy yurt, or dazed by a crowd of shoppers at Costco, I can communicate with my Savior through silent prayers. He has been waiting, waiting for me to realize that I need Him, waiting to offer what my girlfriends cannot, what human communication cannot. He offers me peace! Today, I chose to block out the constant cackle so as to commune with my Savior. As I contemplated His eternal love for me, amidst the splendor of His creation, I was embraced by His peace, the peace that surpasses all human understanding. Thank you, Jesus!

> Blessed be the God and Father of our Lord Jesus Christ, the Father of mercies and God of all comfort; who comforts us in all our afflictions so that we may be able to comfort those who are in any affliction with the comfort with which we ourselves are comforted by God.
>
> 2 Corinthians 1:3–4

YURT FACTOID:

In the late 1960s, Chuck and Laurel Cox, both students of William Coperthwaite, produced a set of plans called The Portable Yurt. During this time, the "back to the land" movement was in full swing, and people were looking for ways to produce their own shelters. Other early yurt pioneers included a Wyoming couple who used the plans to build a yurt community near Jackson Hole, Wyoming, and a hippie tree-planting cooperative called the Hoedads, who modified the plans for forest use in Oregon.

Peek-a-boo! Makai

Jeff Clay, William (Bill) Clay, and Debbie Clay
(pictured from left to right)

Inside Ceiling of the Yurt

Our first ride in Paauilo!

On a ride in Paauilo.

Hello!

A member of the "Turkey Tribe."

Season Three

May–July
2012

Cross Your T's and Dot Your I's

Ten short days after leaving Dad at Crystal Cove Care Center and returning to Hawaii, I was once again boarding a red-eye flight back to California. This time, I would stay two weeks. My hope and plan was to get Dad patched up and moved to a nice board and care home closer to my brother and sister. Board and care homes are wonderful places whereby the elderly live in a home environment while receiving 24-7 care by licensed live-in nurses and staff. It seemed like the perfect next step for Dad's recovery. But guess what? *Life is what happens when you are busy making plans!*

When Pat and I packed up our belongings and moved to Hawaii, we left a car and most of our winter clothing in Moreno Valley at the office of our dear friends, Bob and Sherri. This was to be our hub each time we arrived for a visit. Now, with Dad's special needs, the hub had to change to his residence in Newport Beach. Since Pat had been in California visiting our new and first grandchild, he left the car at an offsite parking structure near LAX. Upon my arrival, I simply hopped onto the correct shuttle, picked up the RAV4, and hit the road for Crystal Cove. I had to see Dad before doing anything else.

At 8:00 a.m., I walked into the rehab center and noticed a beehive of activity as breakfasts were being served, patients were getting ready for a day of physical and occupational therapy, meds were being administered, and God only knows what else!

When I entered Dad's room, I found him sitting in his wheelchair, dressed and ready to go. *Not so bad!* We hugged and kissed, trying to catch up on all that had happened over the past ten days during my absence. Dad's facial droop had improved. His speech had improved. What had not improved was his short-term memory loss, his attitude, or his ability to swallow. After staying for an hour and a half, I gave him a good-bye kiss with the promise that I would return in the afternoon. Sleep had not been my companion during the red-eye flight, and I felt that if I didn't close my eyes soon, I would collapse.

The next three days felt like I was the rope in a tug-of-war game; so much to be accomplished yet nowhere near enough hours in the day. My number 1 concern was Dad's recovery, so I entered the fast track in learning about speech, occupation, and physical rehabilitation. Then, there was the issue of what happens when a patient is on a twenty-hour per day feeding tube—constant urination! With Dad's short-term memory loss, this was like attempting to potty train a toddler. They are constantly either heading to the potty, on the potty, or getting off the potty! With Dad's limited physical ability, we focused on using a plastic urinal while he remained in his bed.

Initially, I tried to cover my father as we maneuvered the urinal into position, averting my eyes, or asking someone for help. Eventually, I just gave up and did what needed to be done. Dad and I usually tried to make light of this situation by cracking an off-colored joke. What else could we do?

Another challenge came in the area of his dental hygiene. When Dad collapsed around his toilet, he not only knocked it loose, he also knocked his lower front implants loose! Five days after I arrived, I had the privilege of carefully guiding him into his silver and black Mini Cooper, and motoring him to his dental appointment. It was the first time in over three weeks he had been free from the confines of his hospital/rehab environment. It felt like we were on *Pee Wee's Wild Adventure.* As we made our way up to the third floor and through the tight turns of a less-than-wheelchair-friendly dental office, I had a newfound respect for the challenges of those bound to roll rather than stroll.

An hour later, we "rolled" our way back to the Mini, Dad's implants now secure and his spirit refreshed. We even did a drive-by so he could see that his duplex was still standing. By the time we rolled back into Crystal Cove, it was "lights out" for the weary traveler. (Dad needed a nap too!)

"Not enough hours in the day" typified my schedule over that two-week period. I hired two house cleaners, working side-by-side, for a total of fourteen hours, to get Dad's home clean as a whistle. I shopped for a new dishwasher, observing its installation four days later. I rolled over a CD, paid his bills, stocked the fridge, and fed my siblings. I kept my commitment to speak at five Stonecroft Women's Connection luncheons, driving over one thousand miles between four counties. And I visited daily with Dad, not only providing love and encouragement but also monitoring his care and progress.

As in most rehab cases, there were good days and not-so-good days. A person's physical, emotional, and mental health is paramount for the healing process to occur. But their spiritual health must also be factored in, not only for the present but, more importantly, for eternity. My brother, sister, and I, along with our spouses and children, have all asked Jesus into our hearts, to forgive us of our sins and to give us an eternal home in heaven with Him. Dad professed this same faith, but we had our concerns. Now that he seemingly had "one foot out the door and the other on a banana peel," as he liked to put it, we needed confirmation that his final address was securely in heaven.

As the days went by his conversations turned more and more heavenward. Prior to both trips to California, I asked the Lord to open the door so I could talk with Dad about his faith in Jesus, to confirm his faith so we all would have peace when the time came, Dad included. Then, one morning, the door squeaked opened...

It was Sunday, May 15, the seventh morning of my trip, when I sleepily answered my cell phone to a somewhat distraught brother on the other end. Jeff explained that Dad had called him at 2:30 a.m. asking him to say a prayer at church that morning for God to take him to heaven! Jeff tried to explain that God would take him at his appointed time, not because Jeff asked Him. Dad wasn't buying Jeff's explanation! Before we hung up, I promised Jeff I would call Dad. When I got him on the line, I asked him about his request. He confirmed that he wanted to go. I said, "Dad, this time with you is special. Don't you want to be with us?"

He said, in a matter-of-fact tone of voice, "I'll see you in heaven!" I agreed and then stepped through the open door.

"Dad, you're the kind of man who likes to cross your *T*s and dot your *I*'s, right? He agreed. "Would you like to be absolutely sure of your ticket to heaven?"

He said, "Yes."

"Okay, let's take care of that right now." He agreed. "I'll lead you in a simple prayer, and you repeat after me. If you don't agree with something, just stop me. Are you ready?"

He responded, "Yes."

"Okay, close your eyes and repeat after me...Dear Heavenly Father [he repeated], I believe in You. [He repeated] I believe in your Son, Jesus Christ. I believe I asked You into my heart when I walked the aisle at church many years ago. I ask You to forgive me of my sins and to take me to heaven when You say the time is right. Meanwhile, please give me courage each day until I go. In Jesus's name, amen."

What a tender time we had together, a moment of eternal importance between a father, his daughter, and their heavenly Father! No matter what else was to happen in the future, Dad's final resting place was secure. And that was all the security I needed. As I boarded the plane back to Hawaii, and every day since that special morning prayer, I have reflected on the miracle that occurred and God's love for His creation, one precious soul at a time.

> Behold, I stand at the door and knock; if anyone hears My voice and opens the door, I will come in to him, and will dine with him, and he with Me.
>
> Revelation 3:20
>
> Jesus said to him, "I am the way, and the truth, and the life; no one comes to the Father but through Me."
>
> John 14:6

YURT FACTOID:

In 1970, psychologist John Nance, and his wife, Pat, moved their family from Orange County, California, to Polk County, Oregon. They purchased thirteen acres of steeply sloped forestland and slowly designed, milled, and built a uniquely integrated three-story yurt.

"Many of the ceilings have interesting shapes. The rooms lay out as wedges, with leaning-out exterior walls. It is enjoyable to live in this space. The rooms lay out pleasantly. The kitchen and living room make good social areas, and the bedrooms are quiet and private."

John Nance

Things That Stick!

Precious Makai, my somewhat rare female orange tabby kitten, is now just shy of three months old. One of her hangouts is on our lanai whereby she is delicately harnessed using a soft white cord. Two days ago, while she sat at her perch and I was inside at my desk, I heard Pat start up the ride-on lawnmower. After a few minutes of pushing papers, I realized I needed to move her down to her nursery, also referred to as our bathroom. (Lawnmowers can be very scary, you know!) I went out onto the lanai and quickly discovered that she was gone, harness, cord, and all! I looked around and noticed that the cord had been tied to a stake in our nearby pineapple patch. Following the cord led me to an empty harness. With eyeballs popping out, I quickly surveyed the area—no kitty!

As Pat came whipping around the corner on the mower, I wildly flagged him down, yelling, "Where's the cat?" He pointed to the pineapple patch. I repeated my question. Again, he pointed. By the third time, reality began to register with him. He turned off the mower, marched over to the patch, picked up the cord, and followed it, only to come to the same conclusion I had—no kitty! My next six hours were spent roaming the grassy, tree-covered hills of Paauilo, calling her name while sending arrow prayers heavenward.

Reality quickly began to sink in. *How would I ever find her? How would she ever find her way home? What about the mongoose, owls, and hawks? She is so little!* I allowed myself to break into tears just once. My biggest challenge was keeping myself from yelling terrible accusations at Pat. After all, who on earth would tie up a three-month-old kitten in a pineapple patch and then happily mow all around it? Eventually, I called all my neighbors to put them on red alert. On my third trip around the area, I stopped at Joe and Kelly's place.

After we unsuccessfully inspected their seven-acre property, Joe announced that he would get his three kids in on the search. With that, I offered a ten-dollar reward if they found her. (I know that sounds a little on the cheap side, but heck, these are kids, and times are tough!) I will spare you the details and skip to the end of the story. Joe's thirteen-year-old daughter, Taryn, prowled their property, eventually spotting Little Miss Runaway in their huge pasture. (Let's not mention the fact that this pasture contained one very large steer named Stew!) Taryn was able to motivate Makai toward the yurt, and with Pat on the constant lookout, she soon popped her orange head out of the Ti Leaf patch that lined one side of our hog–wire fenced yard. Using the white cord as kitty enticement, I was eventually able to grab the missing family member! "What a relief" is an understatement. Pat immediately dove into his wallet and produced a ten-dollar bill as payment to Taryn, indicating, "I think this is my responsibility." Rolling my eyes, I didn't argue the fact.

So now you have the mechanics of what went on during the big search. But what was really going on here? I had actually planned to write on the topic of things that stick. I don't remember the original intent, but I do believe that God had something else in mind. What are some things that stick? Honey sticks. Syrup sticks. Toilet paper can stick. Fly paper sticks. Candy can be sticky. On and on it goes.

A Bible verse indicates that there is a friend who sticks closer than a brother. Is the author talking about a true friend or Jesus? I am not absolutely sure, but maybe both. During the emotional ordeal of searching for my tiny tabby, I needed someone to stick this out with me. Pat was dumbfounded when Makai went missing. He knows how much I love her and how special she is to me. (I think he secretly loves her too.) He hated seeing me in pain as I called for her hour after hour. At one point, he simply disappeared. I think he went off to pray. He stuck closer than a brother. Then, he took up his post at the yurt in the event she returned while I was off on the search. Taryn joined the team. Would I say she stuck closer than a brother? She didn't give up and was even present when Makai was actually found. But I think the lesson here, for me, was to put feet to my faith.

I believe it is Jesus who truly sticks closer than a brother! So I prayed and prayed and prayed. I told Him I knew that He knew exactly where she was, that finding her would be like trying to find a needle in a haystack. (And who is in charge of both the needle and the haystack?) I reminded Him that He had given her to me as a special gift, and I asked Him to help me to not come unglued if she didn't return, as well as help me to forgive Pat.

You see, an orange tabby kitten had become stuck to my heart, just like glue to paper. And as Makai was stuck to me, I was stuck to Jesus. He promises me, "I will never leave you, nor will I ever forsake you" (Hebrews 13:5b, also see Deuteronomy 31:6 and 31:8 and Joshua 1:5). Wow, that is "stuck," isn't it? So as Makai was happily on the lam, I stuck with my Savior while taking the human footsteps toward her return. We all worked together, and eventually the prodigal kitty returned! Who are you stuck to?

{
A man of too many friends comes to ruin, but there is a friend who sticks closer than a brother.

Proverbs 18:24
}

YURT FACTOID:

"In a yurt, you can feel what's going on in the outside. You also become aware when you're bringing in wood for a fire, of how much of the world's resources you're using; you become more mindful."

Dan Beck

Pink Toenails

Pat loves to take an idea, a simple idea, and expound upon it. When I casually mentioned that I thought our yurt was somewhere between 425 to 475 not-so-square feet, he whipped out the calculator and started wildly punching numbers. Something about "pi this" and "square that." I didn't really care how he got the right answer. I was just curious as to what the right answer was. After a few more calculations and more explanation than my pea-brain could hold, voilà! "Our yurt is 450 not-so-square feet!" he proudly announced. (You may ask, "Why not-so-square?" Because yurts are round not square.) Granted, the accurate not-so-square footage of our yurt did not change my day, but in the middle of the night, the reality of living in the yurt posed a bit of a problem.

My friends and family know that my toenails always sport a spiffy shade of pink nail polish. My farrier, Susanella, has even chuckled at me because I rarely wear anything but flip-flops (rubbah slippahs in Hawaiian lingo) even when I hang with Smoke. "Pink toes! They're so cute!" she exclaimed one day. I've had a few challenges with my two big pink toes. It's called fungus under the nail. (Gee, do you think cleaning the horse corral in slippahs could possibly contribute to this situation?)

One night, I was rudely awakened by a pounding sensation in my right big pink toe. *Yikes, that hurts.* I tossed and turned for quite a while, finally succumbing to the fact that I had to get up and deal with Pinky. This was going to be a challenge. Let's digress for just a minute. Remember the blockbuster movie *My Big Fat Greek Wedding*? The father of the bride had the answer for just about every health concern, including the bride's facial pimple—Windex! Well, my answer is unfiltered apple cider vinegar. After all, it clears up a sore throat, Susanella insists I give it to Smoke daily for his innards, and it cleared up thrush, also a fungus, in both the horse and our Nubian goat, Gerdie's hooves. Now, when Pinky sends up a red flare, I soak it in...apple cider vinegar! Now, back to the middle of the night...

When your home is twenty-four feet in diameter and one corner of your bed is only three feet from one corner of your couch, getting up in the middle of the night without disturbing hubby poses all kinds of challenges. Since turning on the light is completely out of the question, I quietly rooted around under the kitchen sink until I felt the jar of "foot vinegar" and the plastic Tupperware container I use for the soaking process. In addition, I had to feel for my special towel conveniently located in a basket under the highboy next to the bed.

Shhh. I kept reminding myself. With elements in hand, I slipped out the front door, our only door by the way, to sit on the lanai bench for the soaking procedure. Once Pinky got into the vinegar, I knew the pain would subside. As I sat there in total darkness, I asked God, with a quiet chuckle, "What lesson could You possibly have in this for me?" No announcement came forth. But as my eyes adjusted to the darkness and my ears tuned in to the night sounds that enveloped me, I began to get it.

It was so peaceful. So calm. So perfect! Forget the fact that I was actually a little chilly—yes, you can get a chill in Hawaii—the night was beautiful. The stars were like a billion tiny diamonds suspended in the sky. As I sat there, I allowed myself to contemplate the creation of the universe, the expansiveness of the heavens, the grandeur of the earth. I was blown away! That night, in our tiny yurt, on an island in the Pacific Ocean, I could have *no* light. But I was familiar enough with where things were placed to be able to navigate and complete the mission at hand.

When we feel as though we have been plunged into darkness, we can't see our way clear of life's circumstances, and fear creeps in, we must go to the "Author of Light." Once His guiding hand illuminates the path, we can boldly go where we have never gone before!

In the beginning, God created the heavens and the earth. And the earth was formless and void, and darkness was over the surface of the deep; and the Spirit of God was moving over the surface of the waters. Then God said, "Let there be light;" and there was light.

Genesis 1:1–3

YURT FACTOID:

The possible uses for yurts are almost endless. Owner-builders can live onsite in their yurt, in comfort, while they build their dream house at their speed. Then, the yurt can become a guest room, office, studio, meditation space, rental, even a teenager hideaway.

Catch the Water

Pat and I mention, almost daily, how blessed we are to be living in our rented yurt! Even though it isn't ours, we care for it as if it is—weeding the pineapple patch positioned directly outside our front door, mowing the rich green slopes of grass, attempting to stay ahead of the armies of ants who try to invade our little love yurt. We feel especially blessed to live in a yurt that includes a wraparound covered lanai, extending our living space exponentially. We even have rain gutters to catch the valuable H_2O that falls almost daily from heaven.

When you live off-grid, water catchment is a vital part of survival. Unless I am mistaken, rain gutters are designed to catch the rain and then move it away from your home, usually into a rock-strewn area. In our case, these serviceable add-ons were designed to catch the water off the yurt roof and covered lanai, moving it into a catchment tank for further use such as watering the garden or providing for our horse and goats.

Our rain gutters, upon closer inspection, did none of the above! The rain gutters attached to the edge of the yurt, consistently dripped at every five-foot joint, sending sprays of water onto the lanai, the vinyl yurt siding, our feet, our outside refrigerator, and our outside furniture. Sometimes, water even dribbled through one of our eight screened windows, creating quite a mess on the kitchen counter or wood laminate floor.

The second set of rain gutters—yes, there are two sets—actually sent an irritatingly consistent spray of water onto our rock pathway leading to the bathroom and parked cars. A light drizzle was manageable. A torrential downpour required an umbrella and goulashes. Upon closer inspection, we discovered there was absolutely no catchment in this water catchment system! The water just dribbled where it dribbled.

During my second care visit with Dad, Pat announced, via a phone conversation, that he was going to "tackle the rain gutter situation." We discussed our options, and then he went to work. For financial reasons, we decided to repair the existing rain gutters, purchase two fifty-gallon gray containment barrels, and then strategically positioned them under the downpour spouts located at the lowest ends of the yurt. Great! Huge barrels sticking out like sore thumbs and creating additional decorating challenges for me! Oh well, we desperately need the stored water.

Upon my return two weeks later, there they were—gray barrels holding water, lots of water! The plan actually worked. Pat jokingly refers to the whole set up as the "Beverly Hillbillies Look." I'm just grateful for the water and his efforts!

> In My Father's house are many mansions; if it were not so, I would have told you; for I go to prepare a place for you.
>
> John 14:2

YURT FACTOID:

Take a yurt test drive:

- *El Capitan Canyon in Santa Barbara, California*
- *Falling Waters Resort in Bryson City, North Carolina*
- *Cedar House Inn & Yurts in Dahlonega, Georgia*
- *State Parks throughout the United States*

Rubbah Slippahs

When you live in Hawaii, the shoes of choice are called rubbah slippahs. You and I might refer to them as Flip-Flops. Or, if you are really old, Go-Aheads. Rubbah slippahs are worn at church, at work, at the beach, and around the house, or yurt, in our case. When you visit a friend's home, you leave your rubbah slippahs outside. A big shindig equals dozens of rubbah slippahs gracing the entrance to the front door. And in drizzle or rain, they don't cause you to slip, are easy to exit from, and dry quickly. I own nine pairs ranging from perky Brighton's to a lime green pair of hand-me-downs. I didn't realize how tired I was of this island shoe fare until I entered the gates of heaven…I mean Nordstrom!

Here's the scene—I was nearing the end of my second California visit to care for Dad when the idea struck that I needed, not wanted, to get to Nordstrom for a bit of shopping. *How many months had it actually been? Over seven since we moved to Hawaii,* I calculated.

I was past due! (The closest Nordstrom to the Big Island requires taking an inter-island flight to Oahu, definitely out of our budget.) So I motored Dad's Mini Cooper to South Coast Plaza, slipped into a parking space, and briskly walked to and through the entrance doors. Ahhh. What a wonderful sight—shoes, shoes, and more shoes!

As I wandered throughout this merchandise-packed department store, my eyes kept pulling me over to the shoe departments, all three of them! While heading to a display six feet away, I caught something out of the corner of my eye. I slammed on the brakes, took a quick right turn, and there they were—a fabulous pair of blush pink wedge heels with an adorable, yet significant, bow at the toes. These were not rubbah slippahs. These were girlie shoes, and it was love at first sight! Of course, the sales associate complimented me on my excellent sense of taste, noting how popular this new arrival was.

"Do you have a size 8?" I asked. He did. They fit. And before I knew it, I was heading out the door, parcel in hand, and a big smile on my face.

My typical cross-oceanic flight attire includes comfy clothing and rubbah slippahs. It's easy to slip off the slippahs, slip on some warm socks, and then nod out for five and a half hours. Not this flight home. The entire attire had to be reworked, allowing for the blush pink wedges to be worn rather than packed. Comfort was simply not a consideration as I could still slip off the wedge and slip on the sock. And it all worked until Pat and I pulled up to "home sweet yurt" in the dark of night.

"Pat, did it rain today?" I asked.

"I don't know," was his tired reply.

"Pat, I need to know if it rained today."

"Why?" he asked.

"Because. I am wearing these fabulous new shoes, and I don't want to get them wet. Can you please reach down and feel the grass to see if it has rained?" I calmly pressed.

He was a good sport, felt the grass, then announced it had, in fact, at least drizzled some time during the day. My mind was like our blender on high speed. I just couldn't take a chance of getting my nifty new shoes damaged by water spots, mud, or grass as I tromped to the front door. For a brief moment, I considered simply removing my new shoes and walking up the lava rock path. *Nope, that won't work. I don't want to step on one of our resident bullfrogs or get wet, grass-covered feet just before hitting the sack.* So I dug around in my carry-on and produced a pair of—you guessed it—rubbah slippahs!

My next attempt at wearing the wedges came the following Sunday morning. It was drizzling, so I selected a tan-colored two-piece linen pant ensemble. Perfect for those blush wedges. *But what about the drizzle?* No problem. I slipped on a pair of rubbah slippahs, not the perfect match to my outfit, and toted the wedges with my Bible and purse to the Mini Cooper. Church is forty-five minutes away, so I felt confident that I could make it from the car to my pew seat, minus raindrops on my wedges.

Alas, it was not to be. The rain pelted the windshield of the Mini as I tried to spy a safe route into church. Puddles resembling land mines dotted the parking lot. *Well, everyone else will be in their rubbah slippahs, why not me?* More than once during our pastor's sermon, I glanced down at my feet and chuckled. Maybe next time...

I don't think I am unique when it comes to making a choice based on emotion rather than common sense. Do you? In our humanness, we decide to wear something, go somewhere, make a purchase, quit a job, say "I do," all based on what we want rather than what we need. We choose to ignore the red flags that warn us to stop, make a U-turn, or slow down. Then, as we look in the rearview mirror, we wonder how we could be so stupid. Whether it is a not-so-bright purchase or a huge boo-boo in selecting a lifelong mate, there is one person who is always there to pick us up, dust us off, and get us back on the right track. As the saying goes, "God loves us just the way we are, but too much to let us stay that way." Boy, am I grateful.

> You shall walk in all the way which the Lord your God has commanded you, that you may live, and that it may be well with you, and that you may prolong your days in the land which you will possess.
>
> Deuteronomy 5:33

YURT FACTOID:

Yurt styles available in the United States include the Tapered Wall yurt, the Modern Fabric yurt, and the Framed Panel yurt.

The Hen Party

My maternal grandparents, Paul and Bernice Gerrish, lived and died in Pasadena, California. Grandma stood no taller than 4'10", had a stunning head of upswept silver hair, and taught piano lessons for most of her adult years. Grandpa, all of 5'6", held a PhD in mathematics, tutoring college students until he was ninety-three years young. He also opened Pasadena's first swim club, teaching the babies how to keep from going under. As a lover of nature, Grandpa had a green thumb, and was particularly smitten with roses. But it was his infectious laugh and playful sense of humor that got us every time.

If we were holding a cookie or brownie and were unaware of his presence, he loved to sneak up from behind us and squish our fingers together, laughing hysterically as the crumbled mess cascaded to the floor. And when the females of the family assembled, Grandpa would quickly announce, in a clear voice, "I'm heading for the garden. No Hen Party for me!" I never fully understood what that little statement meant until Pat and I accepted the gift of ten two-week old chicks from two separate Paauilo neighbors.

While living in Big Bear, Pat and I had assembled a flock of four baby chicks. The "girls" were very friendly and, in due time, produced their fair share of nutritious white and brown eggs. Over the next six years, we would lose one, then another, until finally, we were suffering from the empty nest syndrome. As our move to Hawaii loomed in the not-so-distant future, we decided to wait to replenish the McGeehan flock.

Nine months after our move, the time had come to assemble a new flock of feathered friends. We missed the joy of having our own backyard "Hen Party." And since store-bought eggs command upward of six dollars per dozen, without much of a discount if you locate a neighbor who sells the precious commodity, it seemed the sensible addition to the horse, two goats, and two cats that already shared pasture space with our rented yurt. No sooner had I mentioned to a few neighbors our desire for chicks, did the offer of free chicks pour in.

Four seemed like a good number, but we decided to up it to six due to the probability of attrition. I told our closest neighbor, Bernie, that we would gladly take six of her peepers, females only please. (A rooster was totally out of the question due to the pre-sunrise wake-up calls that are standard fair.) She confirmed what I already knew, "No guarantee they would all be females." But we dove in anyway with an extra measure of faith.

In anticipation of the chicks' arrival one week later, Pat constructed the tiny coop using repurposed materials from the shed and woodpile. After a few days of intense labor, voilà—the nursery, I mean coop, was completed. He jokingly referred to his creation as the "Gilligan's Isle" version. I told him I felt that was too generous of a description. But it did boast all the elements of a thoughtfully constructed space while allowing the chicks to safely mature—chicken wire siding, bamboo corners, pressboard box and ramp up to level 2, a small perch and entrance door of bamboo, wire, and fire hose, all built atop a sturdy wood pallet. A tarp, pitched over the top, would keep the rain out. We were now ready to accept our half-dozen flock of feathered friends.

Just prior to the arrival of our brood, another friend announced that a friend of hers had three chicks in desperately in need of a good home. "If you don't take them, the Mongoose will haul them off," she shared. Those pesky Mongoose love baby chicks, so of course, we agreed to add them to our fledgling flock. The next morning, Bernie arrived with a little sack of chirping chicks. The original four, then six, came in at a total of seven, with number 7 sporting a tiny broken leg. After receiving an arm's length of care instructions, we placed them into their little safe haven. Two hours later, Pat came home with the additional three babies, increasing our brood to ten. Let the Hen Party begin!

Some hen owners pride themselves on identifying their chicks by breed—Rhode Island Red or White, Bantam, Blue Orpington, Ameraucana, Cochin, and Cornish, to name just a few. That is way over my head. I go by color—three blacks, one gray, two speckled, two brown, and two blondes. I didn't want to name them until they were older because names equal emotional attachment, and I was too smart for that! The truth of that statement was demonstrated just a few hours later.

In the early evening, Pat and I made a final trip to the coop to provide a handful of lay mash for the girls and tuck them in for their first night at the yurt. Upon opening the door, one chick flew the coop! We scrambled to catch the wayward birdie, but she made her escape through the nearby hog wire fence. By the time Pat ran to the end of the fence line and through the gate, she was nowhere to be found. We searched and searched through the tall grass hoping to spot her and bring her back to safety. Two days later, after periodic searching, we gave up. Three days later, little blonde with the broken leg met her maker. We were now down to eight. Attrition, as expected, had reared its ugly head.

Over the next six weeks, the girls grew ten times in size, and their constant peep-peeps grew louder and stronger. It was a continual Hen Party! Soon Pat and I realized that the Gilligan's Isle rendition of a chicken coop required an add-on of open, yet protected, yard space. They needed room to learn how to run, to flap their wings, and to peck for bugs and worms.

After five hours of labor, we successfully completed an 8' × 8' cubicle of chicken wire surrounding the coop. A ceiling of additional chicken wire would keep the owls, hawks, and yard kitties from enjoying a chicken dinner at our expense. Little did Pat know that throughout the day, I was naming the flock: our little gray girl was now Pearl, the little brown one would be Coco Chanel, the twin goldens were Lucy and Ethel, the small black one was Ebony, and on and on.

Once the expanded enclosure was complete, we let the girls out of the coop to explore their new world. We pulled up two beach chairs just outside the enclosure to enjoy their antics. At first, they were very tentative about stepping onto the grass. But soon, they began to wildly flap their wings, sampling the grass, and bumping into one another in all their excitement. I could almost hear my Grandpa say, "I'm heading for the garden. No Hen Party for me!"

When Baby Blackie flew the coop, never to be seen again, it made me wonder why she wanted to leave the safety of her sisters and her home. Did she think the grass was greener on the other side of the hog wire fence? Was she discontented with her home, her family, her surroundings? Maybe she ran because she was frightened. Or maybe she just didn't stop long enough to consider the consequences. I will never know. But one thing is sure—I have experienced similar feelings periodically throughout my life. I have thought the grass might be greener in someone else's life, was discontented with my surroundings, even had a dream once that I was a beautiful eagle, and could fly away when fear threatened my life. And I have most definitely made split-second decisions without remotely considering the ramifications of those decisions. You too?

Paul said it well in Philippians 4:11–12, "Not that I speak from want; for I have learned to be content in whatever circumstances I am. I know how to get along with humble means, and I also know how to live in prosperity; in any and every circumstance I have learned the secret of being filled and going hungry, both of having abundance and suffering need." By the time Paul wrote these words, he had been imprisoned numerous times, beaten and left for dead, and rejected by his people. What was his secret? He had learned to be content. He discovered that what was most important on this earth was not important at all. He had a relationship with his Creator, and he knew his real home, his eternal home, was in heaven. Paul was able to take the good with the bad and the ugly—and he found joy in the midst!

In retrospect, it is interesting that a wayward chick can bring to life the truth of contentment to me. During these past nine months of living in our rented yurt, I too have experienced the peace of living in an attitude of contentment even though, on occasion, the thought to fly the coop, I mean the yurt, seemed just the tiny bit appealing! I wouldn't be honest if I didn't acknowledge that I had to make a huge adjustment when we left California—saying, "See you soon," to our family and friends, handing the keys to our home over to Dan, our fearless Big Bear realtor and friend, then moving into a one-room yurt, off-grid, and on an island in the middle of the Pacific Ocean.

I could have thrown myself an enormous pity party, complete with the decadent chocolate cake of discontentment, the dreamy Ice Cream Sundae of discouragement, and games of resentment, anger, and bitterness. Instead, like Paul, I chose to learn the lessons of contentment—to live in relationship with my Creator, regardless of my circumstances. I have learned that if I stay snuggly in the palm of His hand, I am safe, secure, provided for, and loved. My life's struggles cannot possibly compare to those who live in third-world countries or even the poor of America. But in my own life, God has many lessons of contentment for me. Have I learned? Yes. Are there more to come? Absolutely. Hen Party anyone?

> But godliness actually is a means of great gain, when accompanied by contentment.
>
> 1 Timothy 6:6

 **YURT FACTOID:**

Consider a Concentric yurt, which consists of one muffin-shaped yurt tucked inside another, the two yurts sharing the same roof.

The Few and the Mighty

I am an animal lover, as repetitively demonstrated from the time I was three years old and my parents presented me with Callie, my first Calico kitten. Whether it be the 1,100-pound Palomino equine that graces our twelve acres or the orange tabby that prowls the lanai, I am all in when it comes to the pets we choose to own…or choose to own us.

Our flock of chickens are no exception to this unspoken rule. Our initial plan was to have four hens roaming the property eating bugs and ants while fertilizing the grassy knolls of our Hamakua homestead. Our desire to start with a flock of four fuzzy chicks quickly grew to ten little peepers and then, unfortunately, was reduced to eight. This reduction was unpleasant, but part of the anticipated attrition rate of chickens, especially baby chicks. Like a mother hen cares for her little brood, Pat and I nurtured our flock, marveling at the rate in which they grew. Fuzzy down soon turned into full-fledged feathers, while faint chirps morphed into chatter similar to a toddler with no "off" button. Then, one very early morning, Pat and I woke to a different sound emitting from the hen house.

Almost simultaneously, our heads rose from our pillows, and there it was again. "Is that what I think it is?" I whispered to Pat. As we strained to hear what we did not want to hear, the funny sound came again. Hmm.

A few days went by, and I found myself up before the crack of dawn. I wasn't the only one up. There was that funny sound again. I tiptoed out the yurt, across the dew-damp lawn, and over to the chicken coop. Staring at the "juveniles," as Pat now referred to them, I willed someone to try it again. Pat was sure we had a rooster in the bunch. He was also sure it was the largest of the black chickens, the one I lovingly refer to as Hilda. As I stood there in my PJs, it happened again, but not from Hilda. It was little Ms. No-Name, the other slightly smaller black bird! *Oh no! We do have a rooster in the bunch.* I knew exactly what that meant.

Over the next two weeks, both Pat and I heard what we came to understand as a young rooster trying out his "crow" before the break of dawn. Ugh. It was a pathetic attempt at getting the lungs working in just the right way. In truth, it sounded like someone had the poor bird around the neck, giving it the good old swing. This was not a good thing—for the rooster or for Pat.

Pat desperately needs his beauty sleep due to the many early mornings where back spasms force him out of bed searching for his pain meds. Although I was certain it was Little Miss—I mean, Mr. No Name—Pat insisted it was Hilda. That mystery was soon to be solved. After a few more days of careful inspection, we had confirmation that, in fact, both black *shes* were actually *hes!* Pat quickly named them the De Luz Brothers because we live on Antone De Luz Road, and his plan was to collect the poorly disguised roosters and let them loose in the fields down the road. After all, there were many other roosters running loose in that neck of the woods. Surely the De Luz Brothers would be just fine, finding a hen or two, and eventually doing what roosters do.

One morning, off they went. Bye-bye, birdies. And the next morning—ahh—peaceful, uninterrupted slumber. We were now down to six girls, real girls! Another month went by with no excitement from the hen house. We were really enjoying the girls, bonding with them as they grew in size and ability. Soon it became obvious that we needed to allow them to roam the yard. Just like a first-time mother hovers over her kindergartner as she prepares for that first day of school, I clucked instructions to Pat, "Where are the cats? What if the chickens run off? Get the bowl of water out here!"

Initially, the girls were very tentative when the door was opened and unmanned. But soon, they were running around the yard, flapping their wings, and clucking to one another as if to say, "Yippie! We're finally free!" "Okay, I guess they'll be fine," and back into the yurt I flew.

One Sunday after church, as we drove down our gravel driveway toward the yurt, I mentioned that I was glad I hadn't let the goats out of their fenced area. Bailey, our realtor, landlord, and good friend, was on the ride-on lawn mower, happily buzzing up and down the hills, and zooming around trees at the speed of light. Bailey always brings his two midsized pups. These pups love to chase after our two goats until someone comes to their rescue.

As we made the turn into the enclosed area of our yard, my eyes focused on those two dogs chasing our poor chickens. "Pat, the dogs are after the girls!" I screamed. He threw the car in to park as I catapulted out the passenger side, running, yelling, and wildly waving my arms to try to get the dogs out of the open chicken coop. When Pat showed up, I was so spent I made a beeline for the bathroom.

As I rounded the corner, my eyes caught sight of something in the grass. On second look, I walked over and there was one of our precious chickens lying on her side with her mouth gapping open. I scooped her up, carrying her to Pat. With outstretched arms, I said, "Look what has happened!" Pat grabbed her, and I stormed into the yurt. Honestly, I think I was in shock. Soon the mower ceased, and I heard Bailey rounding up his dogs. After aimlessly milling around inside, I finally poked my head out the door, spotting Pat and Bailey inside the workshop administering first aid to the injured chicken.

Would they try CPR? I shook my head and went back inside.

I actually thought it was very sweet that these two men were trying to help the poor thing. Ten minutes later, Pat showed up to announce, "She didn't make it." Well, that was no surprise to me.

"What about the others," I chirped.

"I found two uninjured," he replied. Within fifteen minutes, poor Bailey showed up at the yurt steps. If he had been wearing a hat, it would have been in his hands. I came out, and after his multiple apologies, I gave him a big hug and told him it was just an accident.

"Want to stay for chicken dinner" I asked. That was just a joke, but it did ease the terrible burden we were both carrying.

Later that afternoon, another chicken showed up. *Okay, we're up to three!* By nighttime, Wilma Ruth limped in. *But where is Pearl?*

She is my very favorite, named in part, after a darling little canine my sister grooms over on the mainland. I love Pearl, and I wanted her home. The next morning, I spent time calling for her. Nothing. That night, I continued to call for her. Nothing. The next day was a repeat. And you guessed it—nothing.

By Tuesday morning, after praying for three days and two nights, Pearl was nowhere to be found. It was early, and I was heading to Waimea for a church staff meeting. As I came down the pathway, moving toward the Mini, my eye caught movement on the gravel drive, and there she was—Pearl! I burst into tears, calling her name. Soon, the other chickens came running to greet her too! It was a full-fledged welcome party as she hopped past the open gate. What a riot—everyone flapping their wings in unison. Her feathers were definitely ruffled, obviously spending a few nights in less-than-perfect conditions. She wouldn't let me pick her up, but as she clucked and hopped around my feet, I knew she was glad to see me and the little flock that had become her family.

After the initial shock of the return of our little lost hen, I ran back into the yurt, announcing to my sleepy hubby, "Pearl is back!"

With a smile on his face and in a muffled voice, he responded, "I know. I heard you."

As the days marched by, Wilma Ruth slowly regained her strength and the limp subsided. About ten days after the fiasco with Bailey's dogs, as we stood on the lawn marveling at our flock, Pat nonchalantly announced, "Eileen isn't limping anymore."

"Eileen? You mean Wilma Ruth," I said.

"No, Eileen. I lean!" he responded, with a smirk on his face. It took me a few seconds to get the gist of his humor. "I've been waiting twenty years for that one," as he slapped the side of his thigh.

"Oh for heaven's sake, Pat!"

Now we are down to five chickens—five lucky birds that have been through one heck of a first few months of life. We have Pearl, Lucy, Ethel, Ebony, and, of course, I Lean! What a brood. Any eggs yet? Of course not!

{ O Jerusalem, Jerusalem, the city that kills the prophets and stones those sent to her! How often I wanted to gather your children together, just as a hen gathers her brood under her wings, and you would not have it!

Luke 13:34 }

YURT FACTOID:

The Tapered Wall yurt features outwardly slanting walls. Three plans are available and include:

- *The Little Yurt is 10', 12', or 17' in diameter, and designed to work in conjunction with the larger yurt options. The Little Yurt can be used as an outhouse and shower unit, small office, child's or guest room.*
- *The Concentric yurt, thirty-two feet in diameter at the eaves, is really one yurt inside of another. The inner yurt is raised half a story and shares the roof with the outer one.*
- *The Family yurt, 53' in diameter at the eaves, is a multi-tiered yurt designed to provide a structure that would be pleasant to live in while allowing people with little money to build without borrowing.*

William Coperthwaite

Two Ponds and a Peacock? (Part 1)

Finally the day, the hour, and the moment had arrived! Pat and I met Bailey at the fork of Antone De Luz Road, following him to the not-yet-listed property. Ten days earlier, as we sat in the Clark Realty office, he had shown us pictures of an amazing property and home. It took every fiber in me to hold my excitement at bay. Now, as we prepared to enter through the open gate and lush fruit and avocado orchards just beyond, Pat's words rang in my ears. "Don't be overly excited because it blows our negotiating abilities." That was going to be my number 1 challenge!

As the gravel road crunched under our tires, I marveled at the majestic Ohia trees and the way the sun shown through their sweeping branches. A little farther revealed two separate ponds, both offering park benches for relaxation. (Now that was on my list of "wants.") After a few more gentle turns, the home came into view—a stately, yet somewhat rustic, two-story which seemed to rise to the heavens, and surrounded by equally tall Ohia trees providing shade from the intense rays of the Hawaiian sun.

Bailey explained that a ship builder from Maui had constructed this home back in the early 1980s and that it took ten years to complete. As we entered, we quickly understood. This one-of-a-kind home, really more of a retreat, was fashioned utilizing an enormous Ohia trunk to hold up the sweeping spiral staircase located in the foyer of the house. Each room was hexagon-shaped, sporting Ohia trunk sections at the turn of each wall. The enormous kitchen, as well as main floor master bedroom and upstairs guest bedroom, also featured Ohia post accents supporting twenty-foot turret-style ceilings.

Each door opening was framed in expensive Koa wood, resembling that of a church as it curved to a center peak. Almost every wall included expansive windows offering panoramic views of the three-tiered rolling grass hills and Pacific Ocean beyond. The twenty-five-foot diameter living room featured a huge curved flagstone fireplace with Koa shelving above. And the substantial three ceiling beams were wrapped with harvested wood from Monkey Pod trees.

Aside from the living room and upstairs bedroom, all floors were two-inch boards of White Oak, my favorite! We even discovered a quaint downstairs bedroom with two single beds accessed by a ship-like ladder. I could envision a host of grandkids scurrying up and down that ladder as their imaginations took them to far off destinations. As our eyes attempted to take in the splendor of this house, our hearts and souls told us we were standing in what was soon to be "our home."

A tour of the nine-acre property revealed unplanted gardens, expansive pasture land for Smoke and the goats, a large yet somewhat rickety carport/workshop for Pat, as well as a specially designated corner of the property containing extremely rare plantings of native trees and shrubs brought here through a grant from the United States Fish and Wildlife Service (USFWS). As the owner explained each planting, an ear-piercing scream resounded.

"What is that?" Pat and I said in unison.

"That's Mr. P, the resident peacock," the owner answered in a matter-of-fact tone.

"The property comes with two ponds and a peacock?" we asked. Apparently so! Our tour finished with a steep climb up a second spiral staircase—this one clinging to the outside of the eighteen-thousand-gallon cement water catchment tank and leading into another hexagon-shaped room, located just a hop, skip, and jump away from the main house. I immediately called it The Lookout because it resembled the seven fire lookouts that protect the National Forests of California. Windows on all six sides provided an unsurpassed 360-degree view at treetop level. True to the builder's love of ships, it boasted a raised built-in queen-sized bed with plenty of storage below. *What a great guest studio,* I thought.

We were stunned into silence as Pat and I drove away, barely able to comprehend the priceless gift that had been unwrapped before our eyes. *Could this really be ours? Is this what we have been waiting four years to receive? And could the challenge of our financial situation actually allow us to make the purchase?* Only time would tell.

> Delight yourself in the Lord; and He will give you the desires of your heart.
>
> Psalm 37:4

YURT FACTOID:

The Japanese design technique of using a raised floor and curtain to define private space also provides interesting possibilities for yurts, particularly when combined with the Japanese design idea of creating below-floor storage space where stored linens or bedding, for example, provide extra floor insulation while being stored out of sight.

Pandora's Box

It has been six days since leaving the chaos of California and re-entering the peace and slower pace that permeates our yurt, our island. Even though it broke my heart to leave my ailing, struggling father, and my exhausted brother and sister, I knew I needed to go home, to get some rest, and to gather new strength and wisdom for the road ahead. While in California, my dear and lifelong friend, Sherri, presented me with a belated birthday gift, a one-year devotional by Sarah Young entitled *Jesus Calling*. Although Sherri says she really isn't a "reader," this little powerhouse of a devotional continuously speaks to her heart. And on May 25, it spoke to mine.

You've probably heard, and maybe even used, the saying, "Don't open Pandora's Box." On Tuesday, May 24, I inadvertently opened that little box which secretively contained *big* trouble. Jeff had called to tell me that during his morning visit, Dad had asked him to bring one of Dad's revolvers to Crystal Cove! Dad had spoken many times over the years about never wanting to be a burden to his family should incapacitating illness take over his life. Each time this topic came up, we reassured him that taking his own life was *not* an option for us! We would be there for him, that life was precious, that there were blessings to be had even in the worst of conditions. And most importantly, leaving a legacy of suicide would overshadow all the good that had represented the life he led.

After talking extensively with Jeff about Dad's request, we determined that Dad needed the "happy pill," an anti-depressant combination of medications to help him handle his "new reality." As the administrator of the family, I dialed Crystal Cove for the umpteenth time, tracked down the head nurse, and, after sharing what Dad had requested, suggested they give him the "happy pill." What happened next sent my mind into a tailspin. The nurse calmly announced that they were not equipped to handle suicide threats and that Dad would need to be moved to a different facility! "What?" I sputtered. "You can't move him. He'll flip out. Send him to a psych hospital, with crazy people?" Try as I might, Pandora's Box had been opened, and the lid would not go down!

Within four short hours, Dad had been transferred to Coastal Communities Hospital. We were told that this facility was better equipped to handle his "needs," and that he would return to the rehabilitation center once he was stabilized. I viewed it as Dad being thrown into the pit, with absolutely no rope or stairs by which he could climb out.

I had an opportunity to speak with Dad just prior to the dropping of the "bomb" by Al, Crystal Cove's social worker. I felt like the worst kind of traitor! I struggled to find words of encouragement that would carry him through this next ordeal. My final words were, "No matter where you go, or what happens next, God is always with you." And I hung up. Thankfully, Jeff was there to accompany Dad, trying unsuccessfully to calm him down as fear and anger tightened their grip.

Because I was so far away, my mind began to conjure up the worst of scenarios. I felt utterly helpless, and my frustration grew to a fever pitch. *This is all my fault! Why did I open my mouth? Will Dad ever be able to forgive me? Will my brother and sister forgive me? Why on earth did this happen?* That night, I had the worst conversation I had ever had with Dad. He was inconsolable, felt abandoned by everyone, and very angry toward the new staff. *When will the "happy pill" kick in?*

After I hung up the phone, I was so spent I could barely speak to my husband. So I went to bed. The next morning, I picked up the little devotional Sherri had given me. That day's reading provided the strength and grounding I desperately needed:

> "The world is too much with you, My child. Your mind leaps from problem to problem, tangling your thoughts in anxious knots. When you think like that, you leave Me out of your world-view and your mind becomes darkened.

Though I yearn to help, I will not violate your freedom. I stand silently in the background of your mind, waiting for you to remember that I am with you. When you turn from your problems to My presence, your load is immediately lighter. Circumstances may not have changed, but we carry your burdens together. Your compulsion to 'fix' everything gives way to deep, satisfying connection with Me. Together we can handle whatever this day brings."

Jesus Calling by Sarah Young

As I reflected on what I had just read, I started to analyze what had happened from a new perspective, a spiritual perspective. Hadn't I prayed dozens of times, asking God for wisdom, asking Him to guide our steps, to keep Dad safe, to bring him through this nightmare called stroke? Yes, I had. Was God actually answering my prayers with Dad's move to Coastal Communities Hospital? For the life of me, I could not see it. But..."

{ Now faith is the assurance of things hoped for, the conviction of things not seen"

Hebrews 11:1 }

My faith was not, could not, be grounded in what I was seeing. I had to rely on what I could not see! I had to rely on my heavenly Father!

The following morning, I chose not to call Dad. I just couldn't bring myself to have another debilitating conversation with him. So I waited, and I prayed. Around noon, my phone rang. It was Dr. Shimmerhorn, Dad's new attending physician. I held my breath for what was to come.

The first words out of this soft-spoken man were, "Your dad is fine! He is a wonderful man, and he does not belong here." That paved the way to an exchange of information as to the steps that would be taken to get him back to Crystal Cove and ultimately to a Board and Care Home closer to my siblings. Under Dr. Shimmerhorn's care,

Dad was receiving the "happy pill." And he would have the throat barium test that had been cancelled the day before. As our conversation came to a close, he gave me his direct phone number, stating that he was there seven days a week, and that his patients were like family to him. As I clicked the off button on my phone, I breathed a sigh of relief. Then, I immediately called Dad.

Sure enough, Dad was in the best of spirits. He didn't lodge one complaint, liked his new doctor, and even asked how my day was going! It was the first positive conversation I had had with him in over five weeks! I couldn't believe the change. As I hung up, I wondered, *Was it the environment, the "happy pill," the doctor? Was it possible that this seemingly enormous nightmare of a move was actually God's answer to my prayers? Was this part of His master plan designed to put Dad back on the road homeward?* My spirit and my heart said, Yes! And I rejoiced.

> Rejoice in the Lord always: and again I say, rejoice.
>
> Philippians 4:4

YURT FACTOID:

The Fabric yurt, an updated version of the Mongolian ger, uses modern materials and a streamlined design. The trellis wall still holds everything up, and the roof struts still rise to a wooden center ring. A steel cable tension band rests on the crosses (or heads) at the top of the trellis. The roof struts are notched and rest on the aircraft cable. The acrylic skylight bubble can be raised to increase airflow or lowered to keep heat in. NASA-developed space insulation features a sandwich plastic bubble wrap between two layers of reflective aluminum coating.

The Church Service

On July 1, I boarded yet another United Airlines red-eye flight from Hilo to Los Angeles. Six long weeks had passed since seeing my ailing father and exhausted siblings. But not a day passed without speaking with each of them. The phone had become my lifeline. As I settled into my window seat, glaring out at the darkness that enveloped me, I did a mental review of all that had occurred during my absence. It astounded me! After Dad's casual threat to use his revolver to end his "new reality," Crystal Cove Care Center had shipped him off to Coastal Communities Hospital, a facility able to "handle his special needs."

What an emotional roller coaster that move created in all our lives. But after a two-week stay, Dad was approved to return to Crystal Cove. The only hitch in the plan came when Crystal Cove announced they would *not* take him back! "What? Not take Dad back?" I asked my brother, trying to keep my voice at a low roar. It felt like someone had stabbed me in my chest! Jeff explained that Crystal Cove felt it was not in their best interest to have him return, reminding Jeff of all the "challenges" surrounding Dad's special care. I reminded my brother of their promise to take Dad back just prior to shipping him off to the psych hospital. Apparently, he had mentioned this, but they refused to budge on their decision.

I find it quite amazing that at the exact moment you need help, the path has already been laid to receive that help. Allow me to explain.

Sometime during the first few weeks of Dad's move to Crystal Cove, I received a call from a representative of the International Ombudsman Association. She explained that an Ombudsman is a neutral, independent intermediary between the complainant and the agency (medical facility, in our case) who investigates complaints and objectively determines if an agency has acted in a mistaken, unfair, arbitrary, or illegal manner.

At that time, I couldn't imagine needing such assistance. So after thanking her for making contact with us, I placed her information in an ever-expanding file marked "Dad."

As Jeff was reiterating his numerous conversations with Crystal Cove, my conversation with the Ombudsman representative flashed into my mind. "Jeff, I am going to make a call. You hold tight, and I will get back with you ASAP." I whipped open Dad's file, quickly finding the contact information. In a few minutes, I was speaking with the director of the Orange County Ombudsman Chapter. After explaining our "situation," she promised to make a call to the director of Crystal Cove.

Within thirty minutes, this angel in human flesh called to inform me that Crystal Cove was "thrilled to have Dad back." What a riot! I called Jeff to give him the good news, and we both celebrated across the airwaves. This governmental agency had really come through for us, and at the exact moment we needed them! Whew…that was a close call!

We had no intention of leaving Dad at Crystal Cove indefinitely. In fact, plans had already been made to move him to a very nice Board and Care Home closer to my siblings. Unfortunately, we had to wait ten days as his room would not be available until that time. When that glorious day finally arrived, Jeff and Debbie happily packed up Dad and his belongings, wheeling him out the front doors of Crystal Cove for what we knew was the last and final time. I don't think anyone looked back!

Board and Care Homes are residential homes run by licensed medical staff. These properties have been transformed into comfortable living environments for people needing more care than their family can provide, yet not as much care as would be provided by a hospital. When Pat's mom, Nana, needed this type of special attention, we found a wonderful place close to our home in Big Bear. The experience was so positive that we felt very comfortable in taking

Dad to something similar in Mission Viejo. And we kept reminding ourselves that this was only temporary.

Jeff was in the process of transforming his downstairs guest bedroom and bathroom into a "wheelchair friendly" space. Dad would move there in six short weeks. As I flew closer to LAX and my eyelids began to droop, I thought back to a shocking request Dad had made a few weeks earlier.

"Darling, I want you to conduct a Sunday church service at the Board and Care."

"Dad, I am not a pastor. I've never done this type of thing," I quickly retorted.

He acted as though he couldn't hear me, explaining that he had told everyone, "She is the female version of Dr. Billy Graham!"

"Are you kidding me, Dad? That couldn't be farther from the truth." But he would not give up, insisting that I was more than capable of doing a service and that everyone would be there. *Wow! The pressure is really on. Now what?*

I have to admit that I was hoping Alzheimer's would kick in, and he would forget his crazy request by the time I arrived. After landing at LAX, I took a shuttle to Dad's duplex, threw my luggage into Raider, his silver and black Mini Cooper, and made a beeline south on the 405 Freeway. Through bloodshot eyes, I eventually parked in front of a modest track home giving no indication as to the special care being administered to the six elderly residents inside.

Upon entering, I met Pretchie and Noli, the onsite nurse and caregiver, respectfully. Their warm smiles helped to quiet my wildly beating heart. A quick visual revealed a quiet and clean environment. Dad had been given the master bedroom. As I entered, it seemed less than "master" but nice just the same. There was Dad, perched in a strato lounger watching TV. "Hi, Dad!" I croaked through my tears. After the hugs and kisses were dispensed, I switched off the TV so we could chat. Dad was now off the gastro-feeding tube, and his garbled speech had improved. Although his spirits were good, I was shocked to see how thin he was.

While at Crystal Cove, his weight had hovered around 142 pounds. Now, I wondered what he weighed. The sunken eyes, wafer thin arms and legs, and boney shoulders set off an alarm in my mind!

After visiting for about an hour, Dad began to nod off. I gave him another hug and kiss, promising to be back later that afternoon. His final words to me were, "Darling, don't forget about the church service on Sunday morning!"

"Thanks, Dad. How could I forget?" And out the door I went.

Over the next ten days, my responsibilities included assisting my sister in decorating her new, yet definitely used, doublewide mobile home, purchased for her through Dad's trust. (We were now responsible for his trust and felt the money was better invested in real estate rather than a CD that offered a meager return.) What seemed like a billion trips to Bed, Bath, & Beyond provided us with hours of entertainment and laughter as we transformed her place into a "Decorator's Dream," in Debbie's words.

Then, I would hightail it over to visit with Dad, sometimes taking him for a roll in his wheelchair throughout the neighborhood or a drive around town. I treasured those special times with him. I know he did as well. But the low point of this California trip was the emergency meeting I scheduled between the director of the home, as well as my siblings. We simply had to get to the bottom of Dad's weight loss.

Prior to this meeting, I had insisted they weigh him. The announcement that he was now seventeen pounds lighter came as a surprise to the director, but not to me. By the time we had assembled in their conference room, I mean their garage, seven pairs of eyeballs were represented. Apparently, the director felt she needed support. So unbeknownst to me, she invited her husband, the hospice representative, and her co-director. Yikes! To say there was tension around the table was an understatement.

I know the director felt like she was sitting on the "hot seat." I would have felt the same way if a patient under my care had lost seventeen pounds in a two-week period, and I didn't know a thing about it!

The hospice representative offered a quick review of Dad's health directives. After a few adjustments were made, we switched gears to review his current health and our concerns. When I asked about his significant weight loss, they didn't really offer any reasons or suggestions. We knew exactly why he had lost the seventeen pounds. It boiled down to the meal situation. Dad said the food tasted like "crap." They were pureeing pancakes with eggs. In fact, they were pureeing everything! And no seasonings were provided.

I promptly produced a new menu plan Dad and I had created together the day before. The director seemed surprised yet pleased with the help we offered. Dad needed more of the foods he enjoyed. And he needed them prepared in a tasty, eye-appealing way. He also required more uninterrupted time to finish each meal so he wouldn't aspirate. Once these decisions were made and agreed upon, we asked that he be weighed every Saturday, with the findings shared with me. An hour later, we exited the "conference room," silently hoping Dad would soon be on the rebound. Only time would tell.

One more responsibility loomed in my not-to-distant future—the church service! Every time I saw Dad, he thoughtfully reminded me about the excitement that was brewing as the residents looked forward to my "presentation." *OMG. This just can't be happening!* But on Saturday night, as I wrestled with the reality that Alzheimer's had not kicked in and Dad was not only expecting but depending on me to do this, I submitted, asking my heavenly Father to guide and direct me. I knew I couldn't possibly do this on my own.

Just two hours prior to leaving for the Hilo Airport, I had the brainstorm to print off some pictures I felt Dad would enjoy seeing. I also grabbed all the *My Year in a Yurt* stories written thus far, as well as some Christian CDs. Now, as I prayed for God's guidance, I sensed His desire was for me to share His unending love for Dad and the friends he had made at the Board and Care. A plan was formulating as I realized that this was most likely their final address. Did they know the way to heaven? Did they know how much their heavenly Father and His Son, Jesus Christ, loved them? Was the Holy Spirit slowly guiding them homeward?

The responsibility I felt weighed heavily on my heart, and I soon found myself writing the script for the next morning's service. As soon as I arrived at the Board and Care, everyone wheeled or shuffled into the living room. The two daughters of Dad's favorite resident friend, Maxine, also decided to join us. (That certainly added to the pressure.) I introduced myself and explained that I was not a pastor but wanted to honor my father's request to do this service. They responded with nods, smiles, and encouraging words.

After a quick opening prayer, I explained that I believed God wanted them to know just how much He loved them and how precious they were to Him. Then, I began to pass out a series of four pictures I had printed prior to leaving Hawaii. The first photo was a headshot of my horse, Smoke. I explained that the picture had been taken at his thirtieth birthday party and that I had owned him for over twenty-three years. Dad burst into tears as he gazed at the image. I quickly gave him a hug and the box of tissue.

One Christmas, years earlier, Dad had presented me with a 22" × 28" framed oil painting he had created, which featured a magnificent headshot of Smoke. He had also written a poem, which was carefully typed and taped to the back entitled "A Daughter and Her Horse." I explained to the tiny church service congregation just how much I loved this horse, equating it to only a fraction of the love our heavenly Father has for us.

Next, I passed around a picture of Dad's dear friend, Quig, holding her newest great-granddaughter. As soon as I handed it to Dad, he again burst into tears. As the picture was passed around, I asked what it represented to each of them. They all responded with, "Love between a grandmother and her granddaughter." Then I passed around a picture of my kitten, Makai, sitting in my lap. They collectively agreed that this picture represented love between a person and an animal. (Dad burst into tears for the third time.)

The final image was of my twenty-five-year-old son, Chris, dressed in turnouts, and standing with his crew of volunteer firefighters at the Sitka, Alaska, Fire Station. Dad really lost it on that one. It was unanimously agreed that this image represented the love between a crew of co-workers, as well as the love and sacrifice they make for the residents of their community. By this time, everyone was mopping up his or her own set of tears.

I shared with them John 3:16:

> "For God so loved the world, that He gave His only begotten Son, that whoever believes in Him should not perish, but have eternal life."

Then, I read them my story entitled "Our Appointed Time," highlighting the fact that God had predestined each one of them to live at this time in eternity, to live at the Board and Care Home, and that He has a plan for their future, both immediate and eternal. Acts 17:24—28a was shared,

> "The God who made the world and all things in it, since He is Lord of heaven and earth, does not dwell in temples made with hands, neither is He served by human hands as though He needed anything, since He Himself gives to all life and breath and all things; and He made from one, every nation of mankind to live on all the face of the earth, having determined their appointed time, and the boundaries of their habitation, that they should seek God if perhaps they might grope for Him and find Him though He is not far from each one of us; for in Him, we live, move and exist."

Heads were nodding all over the room. As I moved toward closing the service, I offered the Prayer of Salvation, giving each precious soul an opportunity to ask Jesus Christ into their heart, to receive forgiveness of their sins, and to be welcomed into their heavenly home at just the moment God called them. Everyone bowed their heads. Did anyone ask Him in? I can only hope so! We closed with a hymn, and then the lunch bell rang. Wow! What a morning! What an experience. I was so blessed, so stretched, and so exhausted. But seeing the smiles on their faces, and feeling the warmth in their hearts, provided all the extra energy I needed as I kissed Dad and promised to see him the following morning. God was so good to all of us. And He still is.

Three days later, I reluctantly boarded my flight back to Hilo. I, once again, had to leave Dad in the capable hands of my brother and sister, hoping against hope, that I would see him in six long weeks.

YURT FACTOID:

The Central Asian yurt is dark and womblike. In contrast, the Modern Fabric yurt, with its multiple windows and skylight bubble, feels airy and full of light. Windows can be picture-window size.

Makai on her "leash."

Pat's clever way to catch the rain water!

The "Girlie" Shoes

The Hen Party!

"There is no secret so close as that between a rider and her horse."

This painting is given, with much love, to my daughter, Jennifer, on her 37th birthday, April 8, 1993, so the years ahead will never dim the unique relationship between this very special horse and his very special rider. *William G. Clay*

Season Four

August-October
2012

The Official
Do's and Don'ts
of Decorating
in the Round

As Pat and I prepared to move to Hawaii, the daunting task of scaling down hit me like a ton of bricks. Everything we wanted and needed had to fit into a forty-foot Matson shipping container. I knew we couldn't possibly fit all the furniture from our Big Bear home into the yurt. But I did hold out hope that eventually I would need to fill a home. I am a nester by nature, a collector of vintage this and that, and a lover of eclectic furniture. *Where on earth will it all go? What do we really need? What will I do with all the surplus?* The decorator in me whipped into gear.

Thankfully, God had prepared me for this unique challenge. My thirty years of unofficial interior design training included living in seven homes ranging from a two-bed, two-bath condo, to a 1926 craftsman, to our custom-built, five-bedroom, three-and-a-half bath home in Big Bear. I absolutely love the challenge of a decorating project.

My first step is to grab my pad of graph paper, sharp pencil, and measuring tape. Then, I measure every room, noting all doors, windows, built-in cabinets, and other elements that need to be taken into consideration when placing furniture. But how does one accomplish this task when the structure is 2,500 miles across the deep blue sea?

Recently, as I put the finishing decorating touches on the newly constructed guest studio bathroom, also located on our rented twelve acres, Bailey's wife, Baki, asked about my "training." "Hmm...well...I haven't had any formal training," I offered as I attached a shower curtain to its slightly curved tension rod.

"Really? How did you learn to do what you do?" she inquired.

Feeling like a deer in the headlights, I quickly explaining that it was something I just naturally enjoyed, that I had learned through trial and error, and maybe it was a gift. In the most professional voice I could muster, I explained that the real challenge is in understanding who the client is, their lifestyle, as well as their personal decorating tastes.

"Well, what would you have learned if you had gone to school?" she asked as she assisted Bailey in hanging a "some assembly required" shelf of espresso coffee-stained wood. I mumbled something about color, scale, and understanding various design periods, feeling like a quarterback trying to launch the football with *no* receiver in sight.

Later, as I sat at my thirty-year-old Husqvarna sewing machine, whipping up three window curtains utilizing two water-repellent shower curtains (two of these curtains would actually hang in the shower stall), I reminisced of the unique experience of decorating our rented yurt.

Pat just loves to sing my decorating praises when visitors stop by to talk story. Here's the scenario: They enter through the front door, the only door, I might add. They stop, do a 360-degree visual scan of the interior, and then say something like, "Wow! This looks great." Some are perceptive enough to notice the multi-room concept. This opens the door to Pat's "praise" part. "Yep! She did all this from Big Bear, on graph paper, and every piece of furniture fit perfectly." Then we casually mention the five-in-one room concept. "This yurt contains a kitchen, dining room, living room, bedroom, and office," we say, smiling from ear to ear.

As they make another visual scan, reality sinks in and they begin to scratch their heads. It's true! Prior to our move, I called Bailey, requesting the exact yurt dimensions and any photos he had of the interior. (Thankfully, on reconnaissance trip number 3, we had stayed in the guest studio and had taken a quick peek into the unfurnished yurt.) Let me simply and lovingly say that the pictures he sent were very helpful in viewing the bones of the yurt—size of the kitchen, placement of the eight windows, location of the door—but offered very little in the area of furniture placement and decorating prowess. Bailey was not a decorator, bless his heart! No worries!

Pat and I had no idea as to the length of our upcoming yurt stay. My friend, Sherri, insisted I wouldn't last six months! In my heart, I felt we would be there at least a full year. Only God knew for sure. So it was important that the yurt be comfortable as well as serviceable for the duration of our stay. As I previously mentioned, I am a nester. I determined which furniture pieces I wanted with me rather than packed into the deep recesses of a storage unit. I measured these pieces and then began the fun of creating a layout that would provide for our needs. Seeing everything drawn to scale on graph paper provided me with the confidence that it would actually fit in the yurt. Here are the furniture pieces that graduated from storage to yurt:

- The queen-size bed rather than the king, along with a new woven-reed headboard, compliments of Pier 1 Imports. Snuggling is a good thing!
- The antique oak dining table rather than the farm table. I love the oval shape and the four recently purchased chairs have that island flair.
- Two Bird's Eye Maple chest of drawers for folded clothing, plus the coordinating armoire for additional clothes, purses, linens, and sewing items.
- Our three-person couch, along with two chairs and matching ottomans, both in the island motif.
- My small-scale antique oak bookcase, perfect for décor items and books.
- A rolling rod for our hanging clothes. (There are no closets in the yurt.) This, I ordered from a work resource.
- We sold Pat's desk, and I traded our sectional couch, round ottoman, and matching curtains for Sherri's Ballard Designs white desk, which was an exact duplicate of the one I use in

my home office. I decided to place these two desks back-to-back, creating a tiny "yurt office."

- One small, low bookcase at the end of our desks to hold books, framed family photos, and other knickknacks.
- A small-scale vintage china hutch, purchased from a Big Bear consignment shop, to provide much-needed storage space for our glassware, Franciscanware Desert Rose dishes, assorted coffee mugs, flatware, and cooking utensils.
- An antique nickel heater, embellished with glass jewels at the base, to serve as a tiny side table next to the couch, and a vintage cookstove set between our two occasional chairs, also as a side table.
- Two 5' × 7' woven rugs to delineate the dining room from the living room.
- Thirteen woven baskets and six plastic storage bins to be tucked under all cabinets and the bed.

I am a lighting fanatic! Years earlier, Sherri and I took off for Brimfield, Massachusetts, to attend their world-famous antique show. We could hardly wait to tramp through ten acres of farm fields miraculously transformed into the country's largest and finest example of a shopaholic's dream come true!

Before we left for Brimfield, I noted my decision to not purchase any lighting. (I already possessed more lamps than one housewife could possibly use.) On our way to the airport, suitcase, and extra suitcase with bubble wrap in tow, I reminded Sherri of this very important "shopping boundary." But a strange thing happened as we happily wheeled our vintage shopping cart up and down the ten acres of antique dealers. "Sherri, I really don't need this!" I said as I purchased an alabaster lantern, a glass globe, and three other assorted lighting elements. She just rolled her eyes. So much for boundaries.

Why do I mention this? Because I had the worst time determining which of my favorite lamps would make the cut and find their way into the yurt. How many lamps do you think one twenty-four-foot diameter yurt requires? My answer is six, not including the three-bulb lighting/fan that dangles from the dome!

About nine months into our yurt experience, my phone began to ring, and my Yahoo inbox filled with messages from friends and family, indicating that HGTV's *Design Star* would soon air a segment whereby their three finalists would each take on the challenge of decorating a yurt bedroom. This sounded very interesting to me because I was sure I would pick up some great decorating tips from these "professionals." After all, hadn't they gone to design school, boasting years of practice in the field? I was prepared to be humbled.

A few weeks later, and after insisting that Pat record the segment, we both settled onto our comfy couch to learn from the experts. As the sixty-minute challenge progressed, it became obvious to both of us that these three finalists knew absolutely nothing about the challenges of scale and functionality in a small, circular space. All three "experts" designed a bed situation that resembled an elephant crammed into a tiny pantry. One designer cleverly created a bed on wheels that held a clothes rod behind the tall, flat headboard. My question? Where did she plan to move that behemoth of a bed?

None of the three design finalists included a closet or dresser for storage of personal belongings. One designer did incorporate a quaint seating area at the foot of the bed. She got my vote. At one point, Pat leaned over and announced, "If they really want a design challenge, they should require the designers to decorate the yurt while living 2,500 miles away, utilizing used furniture, and no budget. Now that would be a real challenge. And, Jen, that's exactly what you did!" I sat contemplating his announcement. He was right. That was my design challenge. And somehow, it all worked!

Over the next few days, I went into creative mode, allowing my mind to place me into the HGTV *Design Star Challenge*. How would I have designed a yurt bedroom? This is what I came up with:

1.   Build a queen-size headboard that follows the curvature of the yurt wall.
2.   Add a bedside table and a wall sconce or swivel lamp.

3. Include a comfy chair with ottoman, perfect for quiet times of contemplation or reading.
4. Add another properly proportioned side table with a small crystal chandelier. (Of course!)
5. Small chest of drawers for personal clothing, and three hooks for hanging items.
6. Potbelly stove for warmth during cold evenings and mornings.
7. A microwave atop a mini refrigerator, along with a small table that includes a coordinating array of necessary utensils, dishes, and glassware.
8. Plush rug.
9. Mirror for dressing and spruce up.
10. Assorted baskets for storage of miscellaneous items.

So here is my list of do's and don'ts when designing your own yurt...or small space:

DO:

1. Include your favorite must-have furniture, paying careful attention to scale.
2. Purchase matching baskets that can store socks, craft necessities, kitchen items, DVDs, CDs, etc., and slide them under cabinets and chairs.
3. Purchase plastic storage bins to store off-season clothing, shoes, purses backup necessities for the bathroom, and other miscellaneous must-haves, storing everything conveniently under your bed.
4. Determine a color scheme and stick with it. Mine was red, white, and black, with a few dashes of green, yellow, and pink, just to add some kick.
5. Pair down your kitchen equipment. You don't need every piece of Tupperware and your entire collection of pots and pans.

6. Consider lighting. If your mate is sleeping, where will you read?
7. Utilize the middle of the room. A dining table can butt up to the back of your couch, creating a much-needed dining space.
8. Thin out your collections. Less is more! Pack away the Lladros, Waterford, and vintage glassware to be able to display your collection of Alabaster bookends, bowls, and matching table lamp.
9. Clean out your wardrobe. Again, less is more. If you haven't worn it in a year, sell it at a consignment store or donate it to the Salvation Army.
10. Move part of your kitchen outside, weather permitting. Ours includes the refrigerator, microwave, recycle bins, a camp table holding the small electric grill, and a bowl of fruit. (No lamps!)

DON'T:

1. Try to cram in furniture that overtakes the space. Switch out a huge china cabinet for a more petite version.
2. Go with eight dining room chairs when the space only holds four.
3. Try to tell the story of a three-thousand-square-foot home in a one-room space.
4. Use every color of the rainbow.
5. Forget to keep things tidy. Put your stuff away!
6. Forget your mate. What will he/she need to feel comfy and cozy?

YURT FACTOID:

"There is no particular beauty in a round building—no more than a square building—if the proportions aren't right. The aesthetics and proportion are important factors for me. Some builders can just throw up a round building and be happy with it, but I can't. The proportion has to be just right." William Coperthwaite

Two Ponds and Peacock? (Part 2)

A few days after we met with Bailey to view the unique nine-acre property, we asked him to come over to the yurt to "discuss our options." As we sat on the lanai, sipping iced tea, Bailey explained that the owner was slightly reluctant to sell yet knew the time had come. At sixty-nine years old, he felt overwhelmed by the property. Bailey also explained that his ownership was part of a three-way partnership and getting clear title could be an enormous obstacle.

As Pat and Bailey continued their discussion, I had already begun, in my mind and heart, to move in. Bailey felt the owner would agree to carry the mortgage over a fifteen-year period at 3 percent if we could put 50 percent down. Two months ago, that would not have been remotely possible. But with Dad's stroke and the desire of my siblings and I to invest in property rather than low-yield CDs, the money was actually available. As Bailey drove away, with the promise to e-mail us the formal offer documents, Pat and I were once again stunned into silence. Owner carry? At 3 percent interest? How would we ever quality? In prayer, we asked the King of kings and the Lord of lords to make a way, to go before us in every detail, if this was His will for us.

Patience is not my forte. With my next trip to California just a week away, I was hoping and praying that Bailey would get the paperwork signed by all parties prior to catching the red-eye. A few days passed. Finally, Bailey called to report that he and the owner had gotten into a "slightly heated argument" and "nothing was resolved." My heart sank at this news.

On the day of my flight, we called him just to see if anything was happening. He was happy to report that a meeting was scheduled with the owner later that day, and he would call us afterward. Pat and I immediately went into prayer, again asking for God's favor and ultimately His will. As we drove to a restaurant in Hilo, Bailey called and said, "The deal is on!" We couldn't believe our ears, thanking him for his efforts thus far. Then, as we sat at a quaint table overlooking a huge fish pond lined with lush, tropical foliage, we thanked our heavenly Father while sipping from flutes of champagne. This was cause for celebration! Or was it?

After arriving in California, I was thrust into the twenty-four-hour responsibility of overseeing Dad's recuperation from his stroke. He had been moved to a rehabilitation facility fifteen minutes from his duplex. Although he was receiving excellent care, the to-do list was endless, along with the continued challenge of keeping my mind focused on his needs. During this time, I received a call from Bailey. "The owner just can't deal with everything involved with selling and moving. He is overwhelmed!" (Boy, did I understand the feeling.) As reality surfaced, I felt such a sense of confusion and loss.

What is really going on here?

Later, during what I believe was a divinely inspired phone call from my neighbor, friend and property manager employer, Dianna, she shared a conversation she had had with the owner's girlfriend. "He doesn't know where he would live if he had to move." I chewed on that tidbit of information for a few days, and then I called Dianna back. "Do you think he would feel more comfortable about selling if we offered him the use of the Lookout at no charge for five years?"

"Absolutely!" was her quick response.

I immediately called Pat, sharing the details of this revelation, along with the brainstorm to submit an "Intent to Purchase" letter to the seller. He agreed that my brainstorm had merit, so I called Bailey to get his opinion. He also agreed. The wheels were once again in motion.

Upon my return to Hawaii, I drew up our "Intent to Purchase" letter, attempting to address every area of concern the seller had expressed—either to Bailey, to us, to Dianna, or anyone else in the neighborhood. In my humble opinion, that letter was a literary masterpiece, divinely guided by the Hand of the Master of the universe!

I take no credit. As Bailey scheduled yet another meeting with the seller, we hit our knees in prayer. As far as I could see, this would be our final attempt. But what did God have in mind? Again, only time would tell.

The next day, Bailey called to report that the owner had accepted our terms and was very grateful for our tender consideration of his needs. Bailey agreed to draw up the actual buyer-seller documents, and with signatures and a deposit check, we would open escrow! A miracle was taking place right before our eyes. Being the efficient realtor that he is, Bailey reminded us of the challenge of receiving clear title, suggesting we hire a local lawyer to sort out the details. "Without clear title, you can't close escrow," he firmly explained. Once again, I was already moving in, but we agreed to his suggestion.

Over the next three months, Lynn, our attorney, peeled back the onion of ownership that should have been legalized through the State of Hawaii fifteen years earlier. Although Bailey felt that we would eventually close escrow, he always made the caveat, "If title clears!" As November drew closer and closer, the seller packed up his personal possessions and stored them on the property, per our agreement. All documents were signed, and then, he handed us the keys as caretakers of the property just prior to catching a flight to Indonesia.

The funds were available and wired from Dad's estate two days prior to escrow closing in December. We signed the final documents and became the proud owners of two ponds, a peacock, and a glorious home and property just a mile from the yurt, as the crow flies. The "Hale Hui," Hawaiian for "the gathering house," was blessed that afternoon as Pat and I, along with four close friends, enjoyed pupus, praise, and prayer over what the Lord had done for us:

- A property that exceeded our wildest hopes and dreams.
- A property that never went on the market, turning out to be a "For Sale by Owner."
- A property that was within our tight budget and provided for our needs and our wants.

- A property that never required the completion of a credit report.

In a long, long list of God's abundant blessings over the prior twelve months, this is His greatest example of love, grace, and provision for us. Although we would not move in until January due to major and minor upgrades, Pat and I stood hand-in-hand on the lanai, quietly gazing out at the expanse of rolling hills, stately Ohia trees, and the gentle white caps of the ocean beyond. We prayed a prayer of thanksgiving, and promised to be faithful spiritual caretakers of all He had just entrusted to us—two ponds, a peacock, and so much more!

{
Then I will make up to you for the years that the swarming locust has eaten.

Joel 2:25a
}

YURT FACTOID:

The yurt has an inherent ability to bring people together into a circle, which naturally engenders connection and cooperation.

Noli

I awoke while darkness still permeated our little yurt. Slipping out of bed, I carefully made my way to one of my favorite pieces of antique furniture—a pint-sized oak bookcase that has served as a display for a special selection of books and beloved knickknacks collected over the past thirty years. I was drawn to the newest addition, a wickless candle powered by one AA battery, illuminating an intricate three-dimensional cross when turned to the "on" position. What a comfort this precious gift has been to me since moving from California—a constant reminder of God's love in sending His only Son to this earth to illuminate the pathway back into fellowship with Him. So many times, as I focus on the glow of the flameless flickers, I am reminded of my dear friend, Kathy, who gave this candle to me just prior to our move.

Six years earlier, God had divinely connected us through work at the San Bernardino National Forest Association, and then for eternity, as she asked Jesus into her heart during a phone conversation five years later. She presented me with this beautiful gift as we said our "good-byes" at my bon voyage party. It was one of the many ways she has thanked me for introducing her to her Savior and for the comfort and peace she received in knowing that she would one day be reunited with her husband. Two years earlier, George had entered heaven's gates, freed from the dreadful disease of cancer. Yes, one day they will be reunited, and what a glorious day that will be!

This was my first morning since returning from my fourth trip to California, my first morning living in the yurt and knowing I would never again hear Dad speak of his love for me, share wisdom gleaned from his eighty-seven years of living, or feel the comfort of his strong embrace. As rain pelted the metal roof that covered the yurt lanai, and Pat lay sleeping in our bed just a few steps away, I sat on our couch staring at that candle, more specifically, at that cross. With silent tears trickling down my cheeks, my mind did a replay of the last two weeks—of the abundant blessings God gave to me and my family, of the painful experience of saying, "See you soon, Dad."

What a difference a month, a week, even a day can make in a person's life—Dad's stroke on April 9, celebrating his eighty-seventh birthday bedside on April 26, then seven weeks of rehabilitation. On June 15, Dad moved to a Board and Care Home closer to my brother. He had successfully finished a rigorous physical rehabilitation program at Crystal Cove Care Center—most remarkably walking the hallways and down and up the sixteen stairs leading to the parking lot! His weight was acceptable, and he was feeding himself from a fork and spoon, rather than the gastrointestinal feeding tube. Then, after the completion of a downstairs bedroom and bathroom remodel to accommodate Dad's physical needs, he moved to Jeff's home. At this point, his weight had plummeted to 120 pounds, yet his spirits were soaring.

Seven days later, I received the "come home now" call from Jeff. Would I make it in time?

During the six weeks spent at the Board and Care Home, a remarkably close relationship bloomed between Dad and Noli, his caregiver. Dad latched onto Noli like a barnacle to a humpback whale. "Noli!" he would call out every time the poor man was out of sight. Finally, after disrupting the entire residence for the umpteenth time, we hired Noli as Dad's personal one-on-one caregiver. Aside from his three children and the continuation of his daily dose of happy pills, Noli was the only one who could keep him calm and happy. Dad loved Noli!

When Dad moved to Jeff's house in sunny Coto De Caza, Noli quit his position at the Board and Care Home. He wanted to be by Dad's side 24-7. We could not fathom this kind of service, but it turned out that Noli loved Dad too. Their special relationship provided a huge measure of comfort to all of us as Dad transitioned to his new, and his final, home environment. Our plan was for Noli to be with Dad for one to two weeks, training Jeff's eldest daughter, Courtney, and her husband, Dioni, as to the "ins and outs" of his care. The first five days went without a hitch. Then, the bottom dropped out.

Many miracles occurred over the next thirty-six hours as Dad slowly and then quickly slipped away. I would say that his ability to hang on until I crossed the Pacific Ocean was the first in a series. That first day was spent holding his hand, quietly sharing in his limited ability to communicate.

Late that afternoon, Dad received a visit from Sam, a pastor at Saddleback Community Church. Sam had come, at our request, to pray with Dad and to try to calm his fear of leaving us. During his visit, we found out that Sam was also a Marine veteran. Dad always said, "Once a Marine, always a Marine." Before we knew it, we all launched into a very loose rendition of the Marine Corp Hymn, enjoying Dad's immense smile and laughter. But the blessing came after Sam anointed his forehead with oil. Suddenly, Dad's droopy eyes flew open, darting back and forth across the room."

Dad, are you seeing angels?" I asked.

He nodded in the affirmative as tears flooded our eyes. Angelic comforters had arrived. At five the next morning, I awoke to the eerie sound of moaning from the room downstairs. Dad's pain was severe, requiring heavy doses of morphine. The morphine robbed him of any ability to communicate with us. But during the late afternoon, as we sat around his bed, we began to reminisce about Dad's parents.

We could remember his father's full name – Horace Sawyer Clay – but we could not remember his mother's maiden name. Wilma Ruth??? As we were discussing this temporary "brain freeze," Dad's eyes suddenly blinked open. He looked around and said in a barely audible whisper one word. "What, Dad?" we asked. Jeff leaned in to hopefully understand what Dad was trying to say. Again, the same inaudible word came forth. Try as we might, none of us could decipher that word. By late afternoon, Dad's glassy eyes, empty urine bag, and nonresponsive demeanor told us he was preparing to go. Noli mentioned that they usually wait until everyone is out of the room.

"No way. Not on our watch," we all said.

As darkness permeated the room, we continued to surround his bed, holding his hands, speaking words of love to him, encouraging him to go.

"Dad, we'll be okay. And we'll see you in about twenty minutes!"

The Bible tells us that with the Lord, a day is as a thousand years, and a thousand years as one day. At approximately 8:30 p.m., Dad's eyes once again flew open. As he looked upward, I asked, "Dad, are you seeing angels again?" He nodded. We increased our encouraging words, "Go, Dad!"

At 8:42 p.m., with his three grown children and five of his eleven grandchildren by his side, he breathed his last and final breath on earth. For over a decade, I tried to imagine that moment, to prepare my heart for the incredible feeling of loss I knew would come. It was nothing like I had imagined. Although painful beyond measure, we were all together, each of us confident that we would be reunited in heaven. How did we know this? Because the Bible tells us so! God had confirmed this truth through a phone call prayer between Dad and I two months earlier, and with two bedside visitations by His heavenly angels. Thank you, Jesus!

The following morning, as Jeff, Debbie, and I sat around Jeff's breakfast table, "patton" popped out from someone. "Patton! That is what Dad was trying to tell us late yesterday," Jeff announced. We all felt confirmation that although Dad hadn't been able to speak coherently, he had been well aware of everything that was happening bedside. Hmm.

I find it remarkable that at the same time a person is experiencing the greatest loss of their lifetime, they are also called to muster every ounce of strength they possess to produced a memorial service honoring their loved one. As the oldest of Dad's three children, this responsibility fell squarely on my sagging shoulders. I spent the next night at Dad's duplex, needing some quiet time to begin to process all that had happened over the previous forty-eight hours. By the eve of the second day, I had received no revelation as to the date, time, or theme of Dad's memorial service. With time quickly ticking by, panic began to set in. So I went to my heavenly Father, asking for His guidance, His creativity, His plan. After all, He loved Dad more than all of us combined. He knew Dad from the inside out. At 3:00 a.m. the next morning, I got my *wake-up call* and received my marching orders.

"Leaving a Legacy...Through Service to His Country, His Family, and His Faith" became the central focus of the service. The following Saturday, August 18, at 9:00 am, forty family members and Dad's dear friends, sailed through Newport Harbor, destination three miles out to sea, as we said, "See you soon, Dad!" through our tears and our tribute. The AMVETS Legion of Honor gave the Rifle Volley and Taps. His favorite songs from the movie, 1900, along with the Marine Corp Hymn, "Amazing Grace," Frank Sinatra's "My Way," and Nat King Cole and Natalie Cole's heartfelt "Unforgettable" allowed us to ponder all the memories accumulated from his eighty-seven years on this earth. But it was "Remember Me," by Mark Shultz, that ripped at my heart as I tried to contemplate the remainder of my life lived without hearing him say, "I love you, Puce." (Even now, as I write, my throat is constricted and the tears suspending at the edges of my eyes threaten to fall.)

As Jeff, Debbie, and I leaned cautiously over the edge of the Orca II, sending Dad's ashes out to sea, one more miracle, one more confirmation of Dad's heavenly home, came forth. "Look!" Debbie shouted. "Dad's ashes have formed an angel with outstretched wings." And sure enough, they did! "See you soon, Dad!"

"Remember Me" by Mark Shultz

Remember Me, in a Bible cracked and faded by the years,
Remember Me, in a sanctuary filled with silent prayers.
And age to age, and heart to heart, bound by grace and peace,
Child of wonder, child of God,
I'll remember you, remember Me.

Remember Me, when the color of the sunset fills the sky,
Remember Me, when you pray and tears of joy fall from
your eyes.
And age to age, and heart to heart, bound by grace and
peace,
Child of wonder, child of God,
I'll remember you, remember Me.

Remember Me when the children leave their Sunday
school with smiles,
Remember Me when they're old enough to teach, old
enough to preach, old enough to leave…
And age to age, and heart to heart, bound by grace and
peace,
Child of wonder, child of God,
I'll remember you, remember Me.

The Lord is my Shepherd, I shall not want. He makes me
lie down in green pastures; He leads me beside quiet waters.
He restores my soul; He guides me in the paths of righ-
teousness for His name's sake. Even though I walk through
the valley of the shadow of death, I fear no evil, for You are
with me; Your rod and Your staff, they comfort me. You prepare a table before me in the presence of my enemies; You
have anointed my head with oil; my cup overflows. Surely
goodness and lovingkindness will follow me all the days of
my life, and I will dwell in the house of the Lord forever.
(Psalm 23)

YURT FACTOID:

"The Framed Panel yurt features walls that are pre-fabricated into insulated panelized sections. Fabrication happens in a shop, using volume production techniques that reduce waste and keep costs down. Once the onsite foundation is complete, the wall sections are trucked to the site and pieced together by a company crew. The roof, in triangular-framed and pre-insulated panels, is also set by the crew, panel by panel."

California Yurts and Oregon Yurtworks

The Ties That Bind

In 2004, I wrote an amusing story surrounding the purchase of my Mini Cooper. I would like to share it with you, as originally written. Then, as Paul Harvey, the multi-award winning American radio broadcaster always included in his special segments, I will reveal "The Rest of the Story."

My first exposure to a Mini Cooper came during an overnighter in San Clemente, California. The little bombshell had been on the market for a number of months, but living in the mountain resort of Big Bear, California, tends to keep me somewhat behind the times and ill-informed. Pointing at the bright yellow Mini as it whizzed by, I asked Pat, "What is that?" He launched into a blow-by-blow dissertation, giving its name, current maker and road-race history.

All I could think was, "Wow...I want one!" I then made a mental note to investigate the "Mini" more thoroughly. Within a few weeks, I had gone online to gather all the details on this little putt-putt of a car. Yes, it gets great gas mileage. Yes, it comes in stick or manual. No, you can't buy it while on vacation in Germany because they are now made in England.

I drove a Lexus 300 RX. It was a four-door, all-wheel drive, a good hauler, and very dependable, perfect for snowy mountain conditions. So why was I always thinking about the Mini?

On a number of occasions I discussed my Mini infatuation with my eighty-year-old dad. (We talk about everything!) He was *not* supportive, indicating that the car was too small and, as any loving father might think, "You won't survive an accident!" I took all of this under careful consideration and continued my investigation. Every time I shared a new tidbit of information with him, he gave me the same discouraging comments. So I decided the only way to get it out of my system was to take a test drive. This was a unique experience for me because, up to that point, the Lexus was the only car I had actually shopped for and purchased on my own.

My heart was pounding as I slowly approached Crevier BMW and Mini of Santa Ana, the closest dealership to Big Bear. (Close isn't completely accurate because it's a good two and a half hour drive!) Almost immediately, Ken Feskanich, salesman extraordinaire, welcomed me. I told him, "I am here to take a test-drive to get it out of my system!" He simply smiled. We hopped into a snappy little Mini and took off for a twenty-minute spin around town. (I was amazed at how quickly my stick shift training of thirty-three years ago came back to me.)

Driving the Mini was a complete blast. It was comfortable, had excellent visibility, and was easy to maneuver. Leaving Crevier was such sweet sorrow, as I definitely did not get it out of my system! That night I called Dad, sharing every detail of my test-drive experience. I thought this time he would catch the excitement and give me an encouraging word or two. But no, he held tight to his opinions! Now, what did Dad really know about this whole thing? He hadn't purchased a new car in twenty years. He chose to drive a Chevy Blazer, which refused to accelerate faster than sixty miles per hour, even if its life depended on it. His second mode of transportation was a Datsun (Yes, a Datsun!) 280 Z 10th Anniversary Limited Edition. This was probably a fun car to drive, but it usually sat in the garage. I truly love my dad and I value his opinion. But in this case, he just didn't get it. Why couldn't he understand that the Mini was the perfect car for me?

About six months went by before I got the goose to do something about my car infatuation. Close friends, Bryan and Belinda, indicated that they wanted to purchase my Lexus, and they needed it within a month. This prompted me to go online to see what the slightly used Mini market had to offer. I found one in Newport Beach and made an appointment with the owner. Dad lives in the same city, so I called him and suggested he join me for the test drive. Reluctantly, and with a few discouraging words, he finally agreed to let me pick him up on the way. What happened next blew my mind.

As we approached the owner's home, I felt like a teenager going on her first big date, nervous, giddy, filled with hope and expectation. We rounded a corner, and there it was—electric blue, shining from roof to hubcaps. After a brief conversation with the owner, Dad and I jumped in, strapped on our seat belts, and drove away. I wanted to take this baby on the freeway to show Dad first-hand, what she could do, and that it wasn't dangerously small. (After all, it has six airbags!) At one point, I turned to him to make a comment but was stopped dead in my tracks when I saw a silly grin on his face. It looked just like the one I was wearing! Then, as we started to head back, he said the most remarkable thing.

"Darling, do you think I could drive it back?"

I was stunned but quickly pulled off the freeway to switch seats. After one stall, he was taking us back on the freeway. Within ten minutes, as we were pulling into the owner's driveway, he said the second most remarkable thing to me. "Jen, if you don't buy this car, maybe I will!" I was dumbstruck–this man, who hadn't had a new car in over twenty years, this man who had repeatedly stated so many reasons *not* to buy a Mini Cooper. And now, after a twenty-minute test drive, he wanted to own his own Mini? Unbelievable.

What happened within the next two hours still fills me with shock and dismay. I had determined that this was not the right Mini for me because it didn't have a moon roof. (The moon roof brings a substantial amount of light into the interior of the car.) If Dad was actually serious about buying his own Mini, I wanted him to see all the options. After a quick and lively dinner at a local restaurant, we made our way to Crevier BMW and Mini. Dad looked over their entire inventory, finally test driving a good looking silver and black version, two years new, complete with all the bells and whistles.

Forty-five minutes later, he had signed on the dotted line and was now a bonafide Mini Cooper owner! The Mini would be delivered to his home the next day, but that didn't keep us from laughing all the way home as Dad admitted, "I just couldn't help myself." I smiled the same smile I had seen on Ken's face, telling him, "I know the feeling."

One month later, I purchased my own Mini Cooper from a private party in Escondido, California. Mini Mae, as I lovingly refer to her, is cherry red with a white roof and black interior. I also confiscated my sister-in-law's old license plate that reads "minipkg." What fun Dad and I had as we parked Raider and Mini Mae head-to-head for the first family photo.

Now, four years later, we still love to tell our story. And of course, motoring our Minis provides a constant stream of happiness for ourselves as well as those who point and smile as we whiz by!

Hey, Dad, let's motor…

With Dad's exodus to heaven on August 9, 2012, came the task of dividing up his precious personal possessions. (His Chevy Blazer most likely sits in a junkyard somewhere in California, while the Datson 280 Z went off to a car collector back east, both sold shortly after Raider moved in.) Dad had expressed his desire for my sister, Debbie, to have Raider when he was gone. We all think he made that decision based on my own Mini ownership. Funny thing was, Debbie didn't really want it. Her heart was set on purchasing an Infinity G-37, in her words, "The car of my dreams." After a ton of conversation, we all decided that I would have Dad's Mini.

It has now been eight years since Dad and I collectively became Mini motorers. What fun we had during those years, comparing notes and sharing stories. People just love Mini Coopers, smiling and pointing as we motored by. I nicknamed our cars the "happy cars." Over that eight-year period, my 2003 Mini racked up 106,000 miles, while Dad's, a 2002, only had 21,000 miles! He never went anywhere. So after making the Matson shipping arrangements, Debbie motored Dad's Mini to the Long Beach dock, with Jeff following in his Suburban, ready to take her home. Raider was such an integral part of Dad's life that tears were shed as they both drove away. Dad loved his Mini, and we are absolutely convinced that it added many years to his life.

Meanwhile, back in Hawaii, I casually mentioned my decision to sell Mini Mae during a Saturday Yard Sale Shopping Spree with my good friend, Gloria. Gloria was well acquainted with the "happy car" because her ex-hubby had owned two during the last ten years. Within minutes, she committed to purchasing the car. *Wow! That was easy!* Or so I thought.

As Raider slowly made the 2,500-mile oceanic voyage, Gloria and I jumped through the hoops erected by her credit union. My Mini had to be inspected, valued, documents notarized, along with sheaves of paperwork completed. The Department of Finance, Hawaii's version of the DMV, got involved, requiring proper title transfer from California to Hawaii. Then, two more meetings to coordinate the actual transfer of ownership, and voilà, we were ready to complete the sale.

Finally, all hoops had been successfully navigated, and at about the same time, I received notification that Raider had finally landed at Hilo Matson. Yippie! My girlfriend, Sandy, agreed to pick me up at the yurt, making the forty-five-minute drive to get my new and improved Mini Cooper. So much went through my mind as we made the trip in her own spiffy sports car. Even though Dad had been gone two months, I felt like I was getting a piece of him back. *Would the inside still carry his scent? Would I sense his presence? Were there any dings or dents in this perfect vehicle?*

As we checked in with Matson Security and then drove past the chain link gates, I craned my neck to spot the car. *Hmm…a nice horse trailer and dozens of assorted vehicles, but where is Dad's Mini?* I wondered.

Sandy parked and I quickly walked into the Matson building. As if in slow motion, the representative drug his pointer finger down the long list of cars waiting for pick up. I silently began to panic. *What if there was a mistake? An accident? What if it poofed into thin air?*

Finally, after what felt like an eternity, he made a small check mark, handed me the keys and paperwork, and off I went to find the car. My heart raced as my eyes scanned the lot once more. There he was, his chrome gleaming in the hot Hawaii sunshine. Using the key, I hit the auto unlock button, opened the door, hopped in, and took a deep breath. "Hi, Dad. I've really missed you." It was an exciting yet solemn moment as I put the key into the ignition and started the engine.

Shifting into first gear, I automatically said, "Hey, Dad, let's motor!" And off we went.

What a blessing it is to have Dad's Mini Cooper with me in Hawaii, a gift I never could have expected to receive. Who would have envisioned this car eventually making its way to an island in the middle of the Pacific Ocean? The God of the universe knew. And I believe it is just one more way He has watched over me, cared for me, provided for me. Now, every time I admire Raider's adorable lines, slip into the leather bucket seats, and motor down our country road, I sense Dad's loving arms wrapped around me, seeing in my mind's eye that silly smile he wore on his face whenever our Minis were together. "Hey, Dad, let's motor! PS: I love you."

{ We have come to know and have believed the love which God has for us. God is love, and the one who abides in love abides in God, and God abides in him.

1 John 4:16 }

YURT FACTOID:

A sense of different rooms within a single open yurt can be created through the use of furnishings, screens, or hanging fabric to create privacy.

Hansi

As our year in a yurt winds down, I find I am in a time of deep reflection. So much has happened during this year of transition, both joyous and bittersweet. The promise of a new home, complete with two ponds and a peacock, brings me to a place of utter awe. How could this "new growth" possibly spring from the ashes of financial despair, a short sale, and losing my precious father? What about leaving family, friends, and our beloved Big Bear Christian Center? Retiring from my job with the San Bernardino National Forest Association? Leaving two of our three adorable goats, and Chloe, the seal point gray feline I rescued seven years earlier?

Yet here we are, standing not only at the crossroads but practically running down the lushly landscaped path leading to the next chapter of our lives. I am so excited I want to kick up my heels and take off at a dead run! But I can't. Everything in Hawaii takes longer. Why? Maybe because Pat and I are supposed to enjoy the ride, stopping to smell the fragrant ginger blossoms, and developing relationships along the way.

When we received God's green light to move to this ocean oasis, we agreed that I would return to California to visit my family and friends as much as three times per year. Due to Dad's stroke, I ended up flying the friendly skies six times in eleven months! Was this God's way of helping me in making my adjustment, giving me the opportunity to physically connect with loved ones every one to three months? I think it is highly possible.

Prior to our move, and even a few months afterward, well-meaning friends suggested that I would get island fever, run out of things to do, be treated as an unwanted member of Hawaiian society, and experience difficulty in finding employment. Thankfully, I have experienced the exact opposite. I think my eleven years of living in the resort mountain community of Big Bear actually prepared me for this Hawaiian lifestyle. Let's take yesterday for example.

Saturdays offer exciting shopping opportunities as I motor down Highway 19. Garage sales, yard sales, estate sales, and moving sales often create traffic jams as motorist screech to a halt, make illegal U-turns, fail to signal, and jaywalk in an attempt to find the buy of a lifetime! After making my share of stops, and a few necessary purchases, I found my way to the far side of Waimea. I love Waimea, considering it my "home away from yurt." Located mid-island between the volcanic and resort-lined shores of the west side, and the abundant tropical landscape of the east side, Waimea is a small town with a lot to offer. Our church is there. My high school friend, Gloria, is there. (Along with the plethora of yard sales we enjoy together almost every Saturday.) I love the Waimea Coffee Company—their Jenna Wrap, iced "skinny" mocha frap, and decadent macaroon cookies dipped and drizzled in rich dark chocolate. The restaurants are great, as is the special collection of island gift shops.

Although yard sales are always at the top of my "let's have some fun" list, I drove the forty minutes to Waimea to attend a luncheon at picturesque Anna Ranch Heritage Center, the spectacular ranch owned and operated by Anna Leialoha Lindsey Perry-Fiske until her passing in 1995. This historic gem, listed on both the Hawaii State Register and the National Register of Historic Places, offers a glimpse into the rich history of island ranching dating back to 1848.

Our luncheon was in Anna's Hall, a breeze-filled space complete with wall-to-wall French windows offering a panoramic view of the lush green hills just a stone's throw beyond. Our speaker was international best-selling author, Maria Anne Hirschmann, known worldwide as Hansi. Born in Nazi occupied Czechoslovakia, she was abandoned at birth, raised in an abusive foster home, and devoted to Hitler and the atheistic Nazi System. After the fall of Hitler, Hansi survived life in a Communist Russian Labor Camp, became reacquainted with Jesus Christ, and then immigrated to the United States in 1955.

I had visited the Holocaust Museum in Washington, DC, fifteen years earlier when my oldest daughter, Ashley, and I attended her eighth-grade class trip. I've never forgotten the eight-foot mounds of eyeglasses, hairbrushes, and shoes confiscated by Hitler's army as they ushered defenseless men, women, and children into the concentration camps, and in most cases, horrific death. Yesterday, I wanted to see, hear, and speak with this woman who had survived against all odds. I wanted to receive what she had to share—because life is hard, life is scary, life is uncertain. I was not disappointed.

After I parked Dad's Mini Cooper and was heading toward the meeting room, I spotted Hansi sitting in the passenger seat of a car parked up front. In addition to seeing her picture on the flyer our church distributed two weeks earlier, she had the look of someone who had lived a remarkable life. My interest was further peeked. After I was greeted by smile-filled faces ranging in nationalities from Hawaiian to Chinese to Japanese and a few Caucasians, I filled out my name tag and then quickly perused the stacks of books Hansi had authored.

Our guest speaker had found her seat near the front of the room. A few empty seats surrounded her, so I made a beeline her way. As I introduced myself, I gazed into the eyes of wisdom. After a few casual comments, she mentioned something about Germany. I asked if she had ever attended the Passion Play held every ten years in Oberammergau, Germany. Her bright eyes opened wide as she nodded in the affirmative, adding that, "It will change your life." I shared how I had learned about it in late 2000, had tickets to attend in 2010, but had to cancel because our home had not yet sold. Her enthusiasm confirmed my dream of finally attending in 2020. I enthusiastically shared my love for nearby Austria, having traveled to this magical country three times in the past eleven years. Again, her eyes flew open as she shared that she was an Austrian.

At that, I knew we had a connection. I grabbed a seat two down from her left so I could receive every word she spoke. Her message was simple yet profound: "Trust Jesus with every element of your life." Her life was an indisputable testimony to His love and care for her over eighty-six years. She confirmed that He knew her from her conception, had spared her from an aborted death, and actually many opportunities when death knocked at her door, that He had a plan for her life, just as He has a plan for mine—for yours. What is the secret? Trust Him.

"If the Lord Jesus Christ is your Savior, you can trust Him to be your Shepherd through life," she said with 100 percent certainty. Her second point was: Ask. "You have not because you ask not." Every time she asked her Savior for guidance, clarity, or protection, He answered, whether a whisper in her ear or a confirmation in her heart. And speaking of hearts, this little bombshell of a grandma is passionate—passionate about the sanctity of life and passionate about God's great gift of freedom to every American. "Americans enjoy, but all too often take for granted, their freedom."

Surviving the horrors of imprisonment in a communist labor camp, as well as many years of poverty, allowed Hansi to see through eyes of deep gratitude for the freedom she enjoys as an American citizen. These were the times her voice raised to a fever pitch, she stood straighter, and her hands rose into the air. Her third point was: Choice. "God will not push His way into our hearts, into our lives. He is always there, surrounding us with His creation and His love. We must choose to allow Him to guide and direct our steps. Americans have a choice—to be governed by God or ruled by tyrants. Hansi has lived both realities.

After the luncheon was closed in prayer, I quickly moved back to her table of books, selecting two copies of the international bestseller—Hansi: The Girl Who Left The Swastika. (I purchased one book as a gift for a friend who could not attend that day.) Hansi had offered to autograph each book, so back I went to wait my turn, enjoying her presence once again. Her autograph reads, "To Jen, with love! Psalm 37 Grandma Hansi." How blessed I was, how much richer I am for having met her. How much more encouraged I am to face the days ahead. And here's a miracle, she lives on the Big Island, in Kailua-Kona, only two hours away! I believe our paths will cross again, and again, this side of heaven.

God speaks to His beloved children in a variety of creative ways—through His word, the Bible, His people, dreams and visions, and even in books. When I notice a repetitive thread of wisdom over a day or two, I perk up, wondering, *What is He trying to tell me?* Today, as I read the daily devotional from *Jesus Calling* by Sarah Young, the thread of trust continued…

> October 14, 2012, "Be prepared to suffer for Me, in My Name. All suffering has meaning in My kingdom. Pain and problems are opportunities to demonstrate your trust in Me. Bearing your circumstance bravely—even thanking Me for them—is one of the highest forms of praise. This sacrifice of thanksgiving rings golden-toned bells of joy throughout heavenly realms. On earth also, your patient suffering sends out ripples of good tidings in ever-widening circles. When suffering strikes, remember that I am sovereign and that I can bring good out of everything. Do not try to run from pain or hide from problems. Instead, accept adversity in My Name, offering it up to Me for My purposes. Thus, your suffering gains meaning and draws you closer to Me. Joy emerges from the ashes of adversity through your trust and thankfulness."

The truth of this devotional was evident as I listened to Hansi share her testimony of trust in her Savior. And it is true in my life as well. "Trust and obey, for there's no other way." How thankful I am.

To contact Hansi, visit her website at www.hansiministries.org, or e-mail at hansiministries@hawaii.rr.com.

{
Trust in the Lord with all your heart, and do not lean on your own understanding.

Proverbs 3:5
}

YURT FACTOID:

Rather than divide up a larger yurt into smaller spaces, many yurt owners choose to connect more than one yurt or to use a "satellite" system of yurts, where each yurt functions as a different room.

Two Ponds and a Peacock? (Part 3)

It has now been almost fourteen months since Pat and I set up our home in a rented yurt. Hindsight is twenty-twenty, especially in our case. It is so easy to see the monumental mistakes we made over the four years leading up to our California exodus—so many decisions we wish could have been reversed. We would have sold our home prior to the real estate crash that started in 2008, preserving our $150,000 investment, sparing us from accumulated debt of $100,000, and securing our ability to purchase a home in Hawaii utilizing the profit from selling our Big Bear home.

In 2008, we should have priced our home at "fire sale" pricing, instead of believing that because it was *so special* someone would snap it up regardless of plummeting home values. We would have halted all improvement efforts including repairs to the cracked driveway, peeling paint on the trim of the house, dead flowerbeds, and stable fencing that was falling apart. And we should have saved ourselves so much effort in attempting to refinance. The banks were not interested. But were all the heartaches and discouragements really a waste of time? I think not.

Five years ago, I made two reconnaissance trips to the Big Island—one with Pat and one with my dear friend Belinda. By the end of the second trip, and after seeing a dozen properties, Pat and I found ourselves in escrow. The property included sixteen acres, two ponds, an ocean view, gorgeous Ohia trees, and an artist's home in need of upgrades and room completions. At the time, $600,000 seemed fair, especially since the seller was more than willing to carry the paper and at 5 percent interest over a five-year period followed by a balloon payment and bank refinancing! We named it "Stone Haven," a slight switch from "The Stoner House," based on illegal activity that had occurred in previous years. The seller held the home for us for six long, excruciating months as we tried everything under the Big Bear sun to get our home sold.

One day, we were forced to face the music and pull out. Within two weeks, that one-of-a-kind property was sold. I can't really describe the pain I felt over losing it, for it seemed made just for us. And truthfully, I never let it go…in my heart and in my mind. Over the next three years we would inquire about it, asking if the new owner would consider selling off the back eight acres. During an earlier visit, Pat had even taken a picture of the "prayer rock" he had sat on overlooking one of the ponds, asking the Lord to "make a way," if it was His will. The answer was always *no*.

As time drug on, I vacillated between tears, frustration, confusion, even anger. But when the pity party went on too long, I reminded myself that God must have something better for me, for us. This feeling was based on His character and how He had worked in my life over the prior thirteen years. I clung to the truths I found in His word, promising me abundance, provision, and His faithfulness for all eternity. If He promised to tend to the tiny sparrow, would He not continue to care for me? But for the life of me, I couldn't imagine anything better than those sixteen acres. So I walked by faith rather than by sight.

Bailey was such a good sport, always willing to show us properties he felt would be a consideration, patient to the nth degree when we continued to report that our home had not yet sold. I am sure he rolled his eyes as Pat and I shared our belief that God was in control, that somehow, someway, He would eventually give us the desires of our hearts.

After our fourth reconnaissance trip, Pat and I agreed that there was absolutely no earthly reason to return to Hawaii until our house sold. What was the point? Even though our tans improved, we felt a sense of discouragement. We didn't want to be visitors. We wanted to be residents! Then, after that God-ordained e-mail from John in July 2011, inviting us to ranch sit in October, we felt the Lord telling us it was time to go. Hope for a brighter future was renewed. Within one week, Bailey had offered to rent us his twelve acres and the yurt after our ranch-sitting month was completed. We were so committed to make the move that after only a few minutes of conversation, Pat and I said *yes* to Bailey and *yes* to his yurt.

Living in the yurt is paradise for Pat. (He would be happy in a tent as long as it was pitched in Hawaii and his surfboard was propped up outside.) I, on the other hand, had to do a mental flip-flop. This was where the rubber of my faith hit the road of my heart. I had to decide to leave behind my spacious home, exchanging it for the modest accommodations of a tiny yurt. I purposed in my mind and heart to go where God was leading me, to keep my eyes open so as not to miss His blessings, as well as His lessons.

We had no idea how long we would live this way. There were dozens of times I lay in bed, engulfed in the dark of a moonless night, wondering what would come next. How would we ever get out of debt, $600,000 worth of debt? How would we ever be able to qualify to purchase a home again? Where would the money come from? And what could possibly be better than those sixteen acres?

It was during these low times of emotional turmoil that I had to exercise my ability to shift the focus from what I could see to what I could not see. I knew the Creator of the universe. Everything was possible with Him. If He could create the world in six short days, He could bring us the perfect home, in a way we could afford, and at just the right time. I knew it. I believed it. And someday, I would receive it!

As I mentioned earlier, it has now been just five days short of fourteen months since moving into the yurt. Just yesterday, as I walked away from an impromptu visit with the owners of that pristine sixteen-acre property we tried to purchase almost five years ago, I was finally able to see God's mighty hand of blessing in my life. Just yesterday and prior to that visit, I had completed a meeting with Rene, a wood floor refinisher, at our new home, miraculously set to close escrow in about three weeks.

I realized that God really did have something better for Pat and me – a home that was so unique and a property that answered all the desires of my heart. Through an owner-carry mortgage, we saved over $200,000, and at an interest rate a full two points less. Miraculously, we never had to apply for credit! Unbelievable. Only God could have orchestrated this transaction! It is somewhat bittersweet to know that Dad's passing to heaven was such an integral part of our ability to pay off our final two loans and have the funds to make a 50 percent deposit on this beautiful property.

How Dad would have embraced the home's unique interiors of Ohia, Koa, Cedar, and White Oak wood finishes. Dad adored the ocean, living for forty years only a stone's throw from the waves of Newport Beach, and serving as a host for five years aboard the Royal Odyssey Cruise Ship. Knowing that this home had been designed and built over a ten-year period by a ship builder would have intrigued him to no end.

As I emotionally prepare to disconnect from our yurt experience, I find that I am slightly frightened at the responsibility set before Pat and me. *Can we do a better job of staying out of debt in the Hale Hui? Can we live within our means, on Pat's retirement and my part-time jobs with Home Tours Hawaii and the cleaning of rental properties with Dianna? Can we continue to live without falling into the financial pit of credit card debt?*

Our new home requires a new roof, solar system, electrical repair, water catchment expansion, fencing for the animals, refinishing of the hardwood floors, and new carpet, just to mention what sits at the top of our to-do list. It is overwhelming. Then, I remind myself…if I can live in the simplicity of a yurt, with a bathroom under the lanai, off-grid, and on a very tight budget, I can, and I will, make the transition back into a standard home environment.

Standard? Well, not exactly. We will still be off-grid. And I may not get a functioning oven or new bathroom tiles to start with. I will probably have to say "not yet" as I turn this house into our home. But the important thing to remember is that this, we believe, is our final residence this side of heaven. We have plenty of time to take care of each detail. Meanwhile, I will just take a walk through the citrus and avocado orchards, stopping to enjoy the ponds and smelling the fragrant ginger along the way! God has been faithful. His promises endure for all eternity. He has provided for our every need and at just the right moment. We have been the recipients of His great blessings.

> The God who made the world and all things in it, since He is Lord of heaven and earth, does not dwell in temples made with hands, neither is He served by human hands as though He needed anything, since He Himself gives to all life and breath and all things; and He made from one, every nation of mankind to live on all the face of the earth, having determined their appointed time, and the boundaries of their habitation, that they should seek God if perhaps they might grope for Him and find Him though He is not far from each one of us; for in Him, we live, move and exist.
>
> Acts 17: 24–28a

YURT FACTOID:

"There is a beauty, a wholeness, a magic to round buildings. I think humans have a natural affection for non-rectangular shapes. It's simply more natural to build round rather than build a square building in a round world."

Morgan Reiter, Oregon Yurtworks

Coincidence or Confirmation

Pat sometimes refers to them as coinkidinks—chance encounters, unexpected opportunities, answers to prayer, situations that seem to come out of the blue. A friend of mine loves to say, "Nothing happens without first crossing God's desk stamped 'Approved.'" The beloved pastor of a church I attended over twenty years ago called coincidences "the providential hand of God." After all that Pat and I have experienced over the past five years, and especially over the last fourteen months, I must agree. But can I take it one step farther?

I have come to understand that when two seemingly unrelated situations intersect, it is more a confirmation from God than a coincidence sent down from the cosmos. Case in point: Five years ago, I responded to an ad for a darling "Home for Sale" on the Big Island. The realtor who returned my call was Bailey. We would later discover that he is the go-to realtor for the tiny town of Paauilo, the exact area of the Big Island Pat had identified as having the most desirable weather conditions for our eventual new way of life.

Bailey became our Hawaii realtor and ultimately our landlord and good friend, offering his twelve acres, complete with yurt— Home Sweet Yurt—for fourteen months as we continued to dig ourselves out of debt, learned to live off-grid, and acclimated to life on an island. Bailey was also the realtor who received the call that ultimately led to our purchase of the Hale Hui. Nine acres, an extremely unique home, two ponds and a peacock, to mention just a few of the amenities, brought us full circle, completing God's plan for our retirement years. Coincidence or confirmation?

What about this? Two days prior to my exodus from Big Bear, JoAnn showed up on our doorstep, along with nine of her close family members! This was her fifth trip to "see the house," unfortunately at a very inopportune time. A fully packed forty-foot Matson shipping container sat in our driveway. An assortment of boxes, bubble wrap, and unprinted newsprint were scattered throughout the mostly emptied rooms. Floors, counters and bathrooms screamed for scrubbing bubbles. After all, I was leaving in two days!

With bloodshot eyes, I cracked open the front door. Smiling from ear to ear and with eyes as big a saucers, JoAnn explained why she and her family had shown up unannounced: "I just had the feeling that I was supposed to come over! It's perfectly fine that the place is a mess. We can see beyond all that."

"Okay, come on in," I said as I opened the door to provide a wide birth.

"But you show them around because I have to keep packing." And off she went, family waddling behind her like nine fuzzy ducklings.

A half hour later, I decided to track her down. I was in need of a packing break, and I really liked JoAnn. We had developed a kindred relationship during her other four visits. And I respected her as a solid Christian woman. She truly loved our home and wanted to continue the legacy of service to the Lord within those walls. She envisioned her own tea parties on the twelve-foot deep wrap-around porch, Bible studies in the cozy living room as the warmth of a fire escaped from the antique Birdseye Maple fireplace, Thanksgiving, Christmas, and birthday celebrations with her five children and thirteen grandchildren. She wanted our house to the point she could taste it. Nothing would have made me happier! But the real estate market had been as unforgiving to her and her husband as it was to Pat and me. They simply could not sell their thirty-acre home in Three Lakes, California, or their Big Bear cabin.

As I marched around one corner of our backyard, I found JoAnn alone on the west side of the house. I sensed that she was preparing to gather her flock and head for her small home near town. Before either of us knew what was happening, we found ourselves holding hands, asking our heavenly Father to supernaturally make a way for my home to become her home! We had no idea how, when, or even why He would answer this somewhat unusual prayer. We just believed, in faith, that He heard us and would answer. As the tears coursed down our cheeks, we hugged and said our good-byes, a tiny seed of hope beginning to germinate in our hearts.

Seven months later, our home shifted from a traditional listing to a short sale. JoAnn and her husband were able to purchase it amidst a dozen other frantic offers. Dan, our precious realtor, orchestrated the purchase in such a way that kept the vultures at bay. I will never forget hearing her emotionally-charged voice when she called to announce, "We're in escrow!"

But how were they able to afford our home while their two homes still displayed "For Sale" signs? They knew that once our home was advertised as a short sale, it would go immediately. So they dipped into their retirement account! What a monumental blessing it was to know that the home we designed, built, and lovingly cared for over an eight-year period would pass to a faithful Christian woman and her larger-than-life family—that God's Spirit would remain in that home and that His name would continue to be proclaimed. That short sale was responsible for wiping out $500,000 of our $600,000 debt! Coincidence or confirmation?

And what about our animals? Was it a coincidence that a two-week old goat kid would show up at our friend's ranch within days of our arrival, becoming the perfect tiny pasture pal to our own goat, Gerdie, while simultaneously softening the blow of having to leave our other two goats behind? Was it a coincidence that a starving feline found her way to our yurt, acting as emotional salve on my hurting heart for having to leave my own seven-year-old feline with neighbors in Big Bear? Was it a coincidence that a barefoot farrier lived on the Big Island and was trained to care for Smoke's unusual, and highly technical hoof needs, when I couldn't find a qualified specialist within three hours of Big Bear? Coincidence or confirmation?

I certainly can't ignore the timing of Dad's passing into heaven. All three of his out-of-state grandkids had a plane ticket to come to California prior to Dad's stoke, suffered four months earlier. All three grandkids were there to say, "Good-bye, Bumpa!" During his four-month struggle from his stroke, Dad prayed a confirmation prayer of faith, and on the exact same date that Pat's Mom accepted Jesus Christ into her heart—both through a phone call—both on May 13! And Dad's prudent financial provisions opened the door for Pat and me to purchase a home, with a 50 percent down payment, owner carry at 3 percent, and *no* credit check! Coincidence or confirmation?

I love this one... I signed the contract for the 1st Edition of *My Year in A Yurt*, and placed the paperwork in the mail on August 9, 2012, the day my father exited his earthly glove and took his first tentative steps through heaven's pearly gates. Coincidence or confirmation? You decide...

> "For I know the plans that I have for you," declares the Lord, "plans for welfare and not for calamity to give you a future and a hope."
>
> Jeremiah 29:11

YURT FACTOID:

Bear-proof yurts?

The trellis wall of the yurt will keep you protected, but if bears do rip through the fabric, the component construction of a yurt makes repairs quick and cost-effective. Consider a high deck and use bear boards at access points. Try an electric fence. Store food properly and keep your yurt clean.

Looking into the yurt from the entrance door.

Our yurt kitchen.

The yurt bedroom.

The yurt office.

Somewhere under the rainbow… and over the yurt!

We Break For Yard Sales! Marianne, Sandy and Jen
(Pictured from left to right)

"Hansi" - God Bless America!

Please don't cry for me...
For the best is yet to be!

*But beloved,
do not forget this one thing,
that with the Lord,
one day is as a thousand years,
and a thousand years is as one day.*

2 Peter 3:8

Leaving A Legacy...

William Gordon Clay
April 26, 1925 - August 9, 2012

1900's Theme Song & Playing Love - (The Legend of 1900)

Welcome - Pastor Sam Lewis, Saddleback Community Church

The Marine's Hymn - (Music of WWII, Volume 4)

Leaving A Legacy...Through Service To His Country!
Jeffrey G. Clay

Marine Corporal, William G. Clay
March 26, 1943 - December 21, 1945

• Presentation Of American Flag
• Presentation of Personal American Flag and Purple Hearts

Unforgettable - (Nat King Cole & Natalie Cole)

Leaving A Legacy...Through Those He Loved!
Deborah L. Yackel

Children: Jennifer A. McGeehan, Deborah L. Yackel,
Jeffrey G. Clay

Grandchildren:
Ashley Christman, Christopher Burke, Nicole Udall,
Lindsey McGeehan
Shaun Sansom, Sarah Yackel, Rachael Yackel
Melissa Salinas, Courtney Zamora-Clay, Kelsey Clay, Lacey Clay

Great Grandchildren:
Robbie Salinas IV, Donovan Salinas, Holden Clay-Robbins,
Brooklynn Udall, Eliana Zamora-Clay (due February 2013)

Amazing Grace

Leaving A Legacy...Of Faith!
Jennifer A. McGeehan

Remember Me - (Mark Shultz)
Ashes & Petals - Pastor Sam Lewis
Rifle Volley & Taps - AMVET Legion of Honor

A Time Of Sharing By Family & Friends

Closing
My Way - (Frank Sinatra)

Refreshments
Frank Sinatra Medley

Thanks To:
• Noli Sebastian & Pretchie Mendoza (Dad's Caregivers)
• Sunrise Hospice Care
• The Neptune Society
• Hoag Hospital & Crystal Cove Care Center
• Pastor Sam Lewis, Saddleback Community Church
• AMVET Legion of Honor
• Sharon Johnston, photographer

And, Special Thanks to Shaun William Sansom for having
the courage to enter Bumpa's home, call 911, and watch over him
as the Newport Beach Fire Department Paramedics
transported him to Hoag Hospital.

Donations may be made to:
Sunrise Hospice Care
5120 East La Palma Boulevard, Suite 202,
Anaheim Hills, California 92807

Dad's Memorial Program.

"Home Sweet Yurt"
By Sherri Eaton

Epilogue

*When one door of happiness closes, another opens; but often we
look so long at the closed door that we do not see the one which
God has opened for us.*

Helen Keller

We are just ten days from leaving the cozy confines of our yurt, ten
days away from completely stepping into the astounding gift God
has graciously given to Pat and me. To say we are excited would be an
enormous understatement. We are ecstatic! We have named property
the "Hale Hui", which is Hawaiian for "the gathering place", dedicat-
ing this time of ownership to God, to His plan and His will. Where
the 450 not-so-square feet of our Mongolian-inspired dwelling kept
us from opening our front door to gatherings of more than a few folks,
the Hale Hui can handle ladies' brunches, teas, and retreats, while also
offering the perfect venue for men's gatherings centered around an
Imu—a fire pit dug in the ground for the slow-roast method of cooking a pig or turkey!

The breeze will still flow through the Ohia trees. The sun, moon,
and stars will still remind me of my heavenly home. And viewing the

expansiveness of the blue Pacific Ocean from our lanai or panoramic living room windows will not only continue to beckon us to take a break, grab our beach towels and chairs, plus Pat's 10–0 surfboard and head for the beach, but also remind us that although we live in what is considered the most remote location in the world, God knows our address, He knows us personally. And for the duration of our time here, He has a mission with our names written all over it.

> "But as for me and my house, we will serve the Lord."
> Joshua 24:15

I have received a treasure trove of lessons and blessings during *My Year in a Yurt*, lessons I will gratefully carry into the next phase of my life, blessings I hope to continue to share with others. I have learned that less can actually be more, that what you have or what you live in does not define the person you are. I have learned that God's beauty is everywhere, in the rustle of the wind as it invisibly rushes through the Eucalyptus trees, leaving a pungent, rich aroma for my nostrils to enjoy. I have learned that we can cohabitate with cattle that roam our hillsides, wild pigs that cross the road with their brood of precious piglets, sleep through the cackle of a visiting turkey tribe, survive the painful loss of beloved pets and family members.

I have learned that God truly is in every detail of my life, even when it seems He has left the island for a much-needed vacation. He continues to provide for my, for our, every need…and at just the right moment! I have learned that I can live off-grid. If the lights go out we grab the flashlights. If the water runs low, we skip a few showers, stop watering the plants, or purchase the precious H_2O to get by. That hauling our own trash to the transfer station isn't such a big deal. And living without a dependency on credit cards is not only possible, but responsible living!

I have learned that no matter where we go, God provides friends who are more than willing to wrap their arms around us when we need a good hug; loving friends who fill in the blanks created now that we are 2,500 miles out-to-sea and unable to regularly hug our family and friends on the mainland. Wow! What gifts we have received! Maybe as you come to the close of *My Year in a Yurt* you find yourself muttering, "I want God to work in my life in the same in-your-face way He has worked in Jen's," "I need a miracle," or "Where do I go from here?"

No matter where you are on your spiritual journey, today is a new day. You *can* boldly go where you never thought you could go, taking that first, tentative step, just like Dorothy as she touched her toe to that first golden brick leading to Oz. The difference is Dorothy had her tiny mutt, Toto, to cling to; where my hand is held firmly by the Creator of the universe. Only by allowing God to lead me, to lead Pat and me, have we safely entered into a time of healing, restoration, and abundance.

In 1986, God whispered my name when dear friend, Nan, explained in the simplest of terms, "Jen, you need the Savior—Jesus Christ—the Light of the world." How befitting it is that Christmas is just seven days away. On December 25, worldwide, His miraculous birth will again be celebrated, the greatest gift ever received. The story, His story, doesn't end in a dirty manger wrapped in swaddling cloths. The final three years of His thirty-three years in human flesh revealed His divine nature, His power over sin and death, His sacrificial love for all of humanity. I think back to the story of the Samaritan woman in the book of John, chapter 4.

Jesus meets her at Jacob's well. He asks her to give Him a drink. She is shocked that He, being a Jew, would stoop so low as to speak to her, not only a woman, but a Samaritan! He doesn't pay much attention to the unimportant details, instead noting that the important aspect of this conversation is that He can give her "living water, water springing up to eternal life." They engage in a bit of discussion about "water," thirsting again versus never thirsting again.

She then boldly asks for this water! He ignores her request and tells her to go get her husband. She says, "I have no husband." Then, Jesus lays her life open like a filleted Ahi tuna just pulled from the depths of the sea. She is astounded and embarrassed as He reports to her the intimate details of her life. Then, she calls him a prophet.

In His grace, love, and mercy, He tells her that having a relationship with God has nothing to do with who you are, where you live, or what you have done. It has everything to do with "worshipping the Father in spirit and truth." It is a heart and soul condition. At this moment, He reveals that He is the expected Messiah. She is so blown away that she drops her water pot, hikes up her skirt, and heads to town to tell everyone. And here is the amazing thing about her testimony—many of the townspeople believed her! She was that convincing. They then went to Jesus to hear from Him directly. And as their hearts were opened, they received Him as their personal Lord and Savior!

> "And they were saying to the woman, 'It is no longer because of what you said that we believe, for we have heard for ourselves and know that this One is indeed the Savior of the world.'"
>
> John 4:42

My deepest hope, and the reason *My Year in a Yurt* was written, is that I might be the Samaritan woman in your life—that my testimony has spoken to your heart and soul in such a profound way that you are thirsting for the "living water" that only comes from the Son of God, Jesus Christ. How is this constant thirst eternally quenched? Ask. Believe. Confess.

Ask Jesus to come into your life and heart, to give you the free gift of eternal life, as well as a life here on earth that is filled with purpose, perspective, and power to overcome. Believe that He is the Son of God, born of a virgin, died on the Cross of Calvary, rose from the grave three days later, proving that He is the conqueror over death, then ascended back to heaven to sit at the right hand of God. Confess that you are a sinner (taking a paperclip from work counts), asking for His forgiveness in living a sinful life separated from God. You may not understand everything, but if your spirit is saying "yes," this is the Holy Spirit of God calling you into a new life filled with hope, joy, and purpose. (I have no idea how a *Boeing 747* stays in the air, but I place my trust in the airline, the mechanics, and the pilot every time I board.)

As Nan kept things simple for me, here is a simple prayer, if prayed from a heart of honesty, that promises to guide you into a personal relationship with the Creator of the universe. He will fill you with His presence, heal you from life's hurts, provide hope for tomorrow, and seal you with the promise of eternal life in heaven.

> Dearest Heavenly Father,
>
> I don't understand everything in the Bible, but I can see how You have worked in Jen's life, that you are real, that You are there to guide, protect, and provide. I ask You to come into my heart, to heal me, to give me hope and help, to make me the person You created me to be. I believe that You sent your Son, Jesus Christ, to this earth, physical proof of Your love for me. That He was born of a virgin, died on a cross, rose from the grave three days later, then ascended back to You in heaven. I confess I have lived a life of sin and that, through Jesus Christ, I am forgiven of all my sins—past, present, and future. I ask for the same "living water" You gave to the Samaritan woman, "a well of water springing up to eternal life with You" both now and for all of eternity. In Jesus's name, amen.

Congratulations! You are now a new creation in Christ Jesus. Everything is possible! Nothing, and I mean nothing, is impossible with God. I urge you to purchase your own Bible. (I use the New American Standard Bible.) Ask God to open your understanding as you spend time reading and meditating on His precious word, His love letter to you. Locate and participate in a Bible-based church in your neighborhood. There is strength in numbers, and you will find that as you spend time with seasoned Christians, your strength and faith will grow.

Pray! Ask God to reveal Himself to you in the everyday elements of your life, to open your spiritual ears to hear His voice, and eyes to see His majesty and His power. Just like the young woman who stood at the fork in the pathway of Vern's divinely inspired painting, choose life with Jesus. Abundance is just around the next turn.

> Jesus answered and said to him, "Truly, truly I say to you, unless one is born again, he cannot see the kingdom of God."
>
> John 3:3

> That whoever believes may in Him have eternal life. For God so loved the world, that He gave His only begotten Son, that whoever believes in Him should not perish, but have eternal life. For God did not send the Son into the world to judge the world, but that the world should be saved through Him.
>
> John 3:15–17

> But whoever drinks of the water that I shall give him shall never thirst; but the water that I shall give him shall become in him a well of water springing up to eternal life.
>
> John 4:14

Driving up to the Hale Hui.

A view from the backyard.

The Lookout/Ohana.

Mr. P up close and personal.

Jen and Pat pondside.

The Wrap-Up

Tiny Houses = Big Opportunities!

Little did I know that just three short years after the release of *My Year in a Yurt*, the first and only to-date faith-based book on tiny house, off-grid living, this radical lifestyle option would explode in its popularity. Fueled through TV, magazine, newspaper, and social media worldwide, the concept of "Going Tiny" has not only captured the hearts and attention of young and old alike, but is quickly becoming the most viable answer for the affordable housing crisis gripping our entire country.

The State of Hawaii, although rich in agriculture, pristine water, and sun, is still extremely challenged in solving the serious homeless crisis, as well as lack of affordable housing. Now, as zoning and permitting laws are being reviewed and rewritten, the reality of Tiny House Communities are soon to be more than just a pipe dream. Case in point: An eleven-acre partial, currently zoned for one home and livestock, may have the ability to become a tiny house community of yurts, homes on wheels, or domes, providing a safe haven for as many as forty individuals, couples, and families, complete with a community meet and greet room, shared master kitchen, workshop, orchards and gardens, all off-grid! This concept is not only doable, but desperately needed. Tiny House Communities can provide housing for those who currently live under tarps, in their cars, on a beach, or ultimately would be forced to move out of our state. It is a movement that is growing exponentially, and it is a movement I am thrilled to be a part of!

The Yurt Project, now a partnership between myself and Yurts of Hawaii, takes the concept of going tiny and brings it down to a very personal level. Our goal is to provide a move-in ready yurt for one deserving family annually on the Big Island. It is the only project of its kind! The vision began almost three years ago but is now becoming a reality. Will a veteran, a young couple, a family or senior receive this generous gift?

Proof of the Tiny House explosion is evident in the *Annual National Tiny House Jamboree*. Initially held in Colorado Springs, Colorado, in 2015 and 2016, with forty-five thousand and sixty thousand visitors respectfully, it has now moved to the enormous Arlington Convention Center in Arlington, Texas. The annual event offers examples of every type of tiny house imaginable, plus suppliers, workshops, and presents. I was thrilled to be a presenter and exhibitor at the 3rd Annual Tiny House Jamboree, for October 27–29, 2017. For the most up-to-date information, go to www.tinyhousejamboree. com.

Room2Room = Room2Grow!

When Pat and I made our oceanic move-of-faith, friends and family were concerned that I would be unable to find employment. So *not* true! There is more to do here than I could possibly accomplish in a lifetime. Remember the story of meeting Dianna in "The Property Manager" (Season Two)? She did such a good job training me that I decided to start my own cleaning, decorating, organizing, and move management company. *Room2Room* focuses on clients on the Hamakua Coast, many whom are elderly or have serious physical challenges. What a blessing this is to me! And, I will soon have my real estate license, able to give to others what Bailey, our realtor and friend, gave to us.

And that sporty Mini Cooper I used to drive? First, my own red hot number and then Dad's silver version—"The Ties That Bind" (Season Four)? A trip to California, driving my daughter's Lexus 350, coupled with yet another washed out gravel road at home, propelled me into selling Dad's spiffy sports car, and opting for a serviceable Nissan Rogue named Rita. With my cleaning supplies tucked in the back, I can safely navigate just about any road on our island…including my own!

The Christian Women's Gathering = Annual Unity and Encouragement!

In the story "I'm Free" (Season One), I shared about the annual Christian Women's Gathering and the amazing, God-inspired painting I won. That beautiful reminder of God's plan for Pat and me now sits atop our vintage china hutch in the kitchen of our new, yet gently-used, home. After three years of waiting for the "green light," the Christian Women's Gathering/Hawaii will celebrate its 4th Annual Event in February 2018, bringing women from churches across our island, state, and country together for a day of unity, teaching, worship, and inspiration. What a privilege it is to witness God's creative method in bringing His beloved women together. Go to www.christianwomensgathering.com for the most up-to-date event details.

A New Pup and Ferrel Feline = Loads of Love!

Many readers have asked about Smoke, my Palomino Appaloosa flown over from California at the tender age of twenty-nine. I am happy to share that on Saturday, May 13, 2017, we celebrated this amazing equine's thirty-fifth birthday with an authentic backyard luau! Yes, he is still with me/us, enjoying the abundant green grasses of the Hamakua Coast. I have retired him from service, opting to enjoy slower hand-led strolls through our citrus and avocado orchards, while stopping to smell the fragrant Mock Orange blossoms along the way. We still enjoy a dip in the lower pond, often accompanied by Lehua the Labrador. And suffice it to say, we have increased our "herd" of pets, adding Wally, a mixed breed Labrador, and Tucker, a fabulous gray tabby feral cat turned "lump of love!" And Mr. P, our peacock? I am sad to report that he has gone to peacock heaven. We definitely miss the gift of having such a unique animal roaming our property.

When I started this tiny house journey, it truly was a step-of-faith. Now, as I look in the rear view mirror of our lives, I can see

God's hand upon Pat and me in the most remarkable ways. His plan is never just about us. Instead, He sends His loving *tentacles* through us and out to others who can be blessed along the way. This is what Pat and I have witnessed over the past six years of living in this paradise we now call home. If we let Him, He will take all that has been lost, all that has been taken, all that has caused us pain and suffering, and turn it into something remarkably wonderful! But we have to be willing to place our *tiny* hand into His gigantic one, to allow Him to take us where we never dreamed of going, equip us to do what we never envisioned we could accomplish, open our hearts and minds and souls and spirits to receive "a new thing" in our lives. This is the journey we continue to walk.

> Now to Him who is able to do exceeding abundantly beyond all that we ask or think, according to the power that works within us, to Him be the glory in the church and in Christ Jesus to all generations forever and ever. Amen. Ephesians 3:20–21

Yurt Resource Guide

YURTS

Modern Fabric Yurts

Blue Mountain Yurts
02 735 53 097
www.bluemountainyurts.com
contact@bluemountainyurts.com
Yurt sales and support serving throughout Australia, New Zealand
and the Pacific region, with standard yurts in a range of sizes and
custom options. (Yurts provided by Colorado Yurt Company)

Blue Ridge Yurts
Kathy Anderson
369 Parkway Lane South
Floyd, Virginia 24091
540.745.7458
www.blueridgeyurts.com
kathy@blueridgeyurts.com
Fast, affordable shelters for a variety of uses.

Blue Spruce Enterprise
613.824.0839
www.blue-spruce.ca
yurts@blue-spruce.ca
Authorized Yurtco dealer for Eastern Canada.
Located in Ontario, Canada.

Buffalo Mountain Yurts
276.266.6109
www.buffalomtnyurts.com
buffaloman@swva.net
A family-owned business located in the mountains of Virginia.

Clean Air Yurts
30 Crispell Lane
New Paltz, New York 12561
845.633.2875
www.cleanairyurts.com
matt@cleanairyurts.com
Custom yurt homes designed for the future and built
to last. We are also the industry's leading makers
of ultra-light yurts for those on the go.

Colorado Yurt Company
P.O. Box 1626
28 W. South 4th Street
Montrose, Colorado 81401
800.288.3190 • 970.240.2111
www.coloradoyurt.com
ivy@coloradoyurt.com
Building yurts, tipis and cabin tents since 1976. Generous
standard features, durable construction and fully
engineered designs. Shipping available world-wide!

GoYurt Shelters
1.877.4GOYURT
www.goyurt.com
info@goyurt.com
Portable yurts that can be set up by two people in thirty minutes.

Laurel Nest Yurts
49 Watagnee Trail
Horse Shoe, North Carolina 28742
877.326.9878
www.laurelnest.com
info@laurelnest.com
Providing canvas covered yurts, support services, and
assistance for do-it-yourself yurt builders.

Medicine Circle Eco-Retreat
David Kirchhof
P. O. Box 1479
Priest River, Idaho 83856
208.448.1305
www.themedicinecircle.org
medicinecircle@gmail.com
Six yurt styles including Mongolian, tapered wall, fabric and
frame panel "pallet," made from recycled materials. Regional
services include overnight stay or day tour of yurts, building
of frame panel yurts, building of deck/platforms and set-up
of fabric yurts, as well as yurt-building workshops.

Nomad Shelter
331 Sterling Highway
Homer, Alaska 99603
907.235.0132
www.nomadshelter.com
nomadshelter@gmail.com
Yurts designed for the Alaskan market with Lexan panel skylights,
central stove placement and added insulation packages.

Ohana Yurts
Nathan and Jenny Tolar
58-121 Kaunala St.
Haleiwa, Hawaii 96712
808.256.0559
ohanayurt.com
sales@ohanayurts.com
Locally owned and operated on the North Shore of Oahu,
Ohana Yurts has been building yurts in Hawaii for seven
years. All yurts are handmade with the best materials in
the industry and come fully upgraded with taller walls,
panoramic windows, and standard door heights.

Outback Yurts
P.O. Box 58
Stanley, Idaho 83278
208.559.7590
www.sawtoothoutback.com
kirk@sawtoothoutback.com
Custom backcountry yurts with hand-peeled Lodgepole pine
rafters, designed for heavy snow loads. Established in 1978.

Pacific Yurts, Inc.
77456 Hwy. 99 South
Cottage Grove, Oregon 97424
800.944.0240 • 541.942.9435
www.yurts.com
info@yurts.com
Largest manufacturer of modern fabric yurts
worldwide since 1978. A leader in innovation with
options for a wide variety of climates and uses.

Rainier Yurts

18375 Olympic Ave.
South Seattle, Washington 98188
800.869.7162 • 425.981.1203
www.rainieryurts.com
sales@rainieryurts.com
Major manufacturer of fabric yurts, known for finely crafted
woodwork and interchangeable wall panels. Includes a
line designed for camping and backyard uses. Yurt options
include interchangeable wall panels and framed windows.

Red Sky Shelters

Peter Belt
2002 Riverside Drive 42h
Asheville, North Carolina 28804
828.258.8417
www.redskyshelters.com
redskyshelters@gmail.com
Home of the "Yome", part yurt, part dome!
The affordable, portable living shelter.

Red Mountain Lodge Works

Lake City, Colorado
970.944.2269
www.hinsdalehauteroute.org
grayj@lakecity.net
Solar yurts with clear south-facing panels and
clip-in insulation, used on the highest elevation
hut-to-hut ski route in North America.

The Really Interesting Tent Company
Berry Park, Dainton
Devon, United Kingdom TQ12 5TZ
44 0 1803 873297 or 44 0 7843 447603
www.thereallyinterestingtentcompany.co.uk
info@thereallyinterestingtentcompany.co.uk
Constructed from clear treated timber (Redwood) and 2oz poly cotton canvas, rot-proofed and fire-retardant, and is waterproofed to a hydrostatic head of 60cm. Our yurts come in sizes from 10" in diameter up to, at present, 44", and can be used for a multitude of purposes, including bedrooms! So far they have been bedrooms, art studios and galleries, offices, workshops, and even a cricket pavillion!

Shelter Designs, LLC
Hayes Daniel
101 N. Johnson St.
Missoula, Montana 59801
www.shelterdesigns.net
info@shelterdesigns.net
406-721-9878
Handmade yurts and flagship "Eco Yurt" using local sustainably-harvested lumber and eco-friendly materials.

Solongos Camp
289 Sang-Ri, Bongdam-Eup
Hwasung-City, Kyunggi-Do, Korea
82 31 355 8030
www.solongoscamp.com
wellup@solongoscamp.com
Modern fabric yurts for the Southeast Asian market.

Weatherport Yurts
Worldwide Headquarters
Weatherport Shelter Systems
1860 1600 Road
Delta, Colorado 81416
Washington Office
Weatherport Shelter Systems
205 Lake Street South, Suite 300
Kirkland, Washington 98033
970.399.5909
www.weatherport.com
info@weatherport.com
Frames are made from metal and engineered to withstand
110 MPH winds and 40 pounds PSF of snow load.

White Mountain Yurts
Paul Desrochers
43 Bryant Road
Wolfeboro, New Hampshire 03894
603.396.9222 • 877.855.YURT
www.whitemountainyurts.com
info@whitemountainyurts.com
Dedicated to providing quality, hand-built yurts that stand the
test of time. Each yurt is individually crafted, with continued
support from the initial yurt raising well into the future.

Wildwood Yurts
Chris Henry
Wildwood (Cumbria), Fieldhead Farm, Great Strickland,
Nr Penrith, Cumbria, CA10 3DU United Kingdom
01931 712804 or 077868 64516
www.wildwoodyurts.com
chris@wildwoodcumbria.com
Mongolian-style yurts for sale and hire in two designs:
substantial version for permanent applications,
and a lighter version for portability.

Yourte.ca
Saint-Nicholas
Quebec, Canada
418.907.9155 (Quebec)
514.907.4500 (Montreal)
www.yourte.ca
info@yourte.ca
Specializing in high quality yurts using
technologically advanced materials.

Yourte Comporaine
Saint Gilles Croix de Vie, France
33 0 8 73 76 59 51 (Prix d'un appel local)
www.yourte-contemporaine.fr
t.rouelle@yourte-contemporaine.fr

The Yurt Workshop
Rob Matthews
21 Calle Baja
Cadiar, Granada, 18448 Spain
44 20 8123 6241 • 34 622 045 789
www.yurtworkshop.com
rob@yurtworkshop.com
Mongolian, Turkey & Iranian yurts. Extensive website.

Yurtastic
Richard Lee
1518 Somona Blvd, Vallejo, California 94590
415.621.2738
www.yurtasticyurts.com
zensella@earthlink.net
Offering a modern twist on the Traditional yurt.

Yurts of Hawaii, LLC
Melissa Fletcher
P.O.Box 1394, Volcano, Hawaii 96785
808.968.1483 • 808.895.8640
www.yurtsofhawaii.com
yurtshawaii@gmail.com
Our company offers some of the highest quality, most affordable
yurts available, each one designed and custom-made by Colorado
Yurt Company. These yurts are undeniably among the best in
the industry, and include our custom CORR bracket system,
easy to clean and functional cistern system, wide color and
material palettes, custom wall lacing system, and wonderfully
tight-fitting walls. We have a great warranty, and also offer yurt
assembly, drafting and permitting, project management, and
assistance for all phases of the build. We work with our clients to
design a yurt best-suited to their individual needs and budget!

Yurta
Larkland Highlands, Quebec
877.807.5008 • 905.831.0418
www.yurta.ca
info@yurta.ca
An original design developed to provide a strong yet truly
portable dwelling that is rooted in nomadic tradition.

Yurts of America
4375 Sellers Street
Indianapolis, Indiana
317.377.9879
www.yurtsofamerica.com
info@yurtsofamerica.com
Certified engineering, quality craftsmanship, and durable materials *guaranteed*. Yurts of America offers the best and most economical year-round yurt on the market today.

Yurtz by Design
20673 Langley Bypass
Langley BC V3A 5E8
604.576.9878 • 855.576.9878
www.yurtzbydesign.com
info@yurtzbydesign.com
Canada's number one yurt manufacturer.

Traditional Yurts

Adorjan Yurts
36 0 27-383 • 36 0 30 445 0780
www.adorjan-jurta.hu
info@adorjan-jurta.hu
Mongolian-style yurts handmade in Hungary.

Albion Canvas Company
Unit 6, Barkingdon Business Park Staverton, Totnes
Devon, UK TQ9 6AN
0845.456.9290 (local rate) • 44 0 1803 762230
www.albioncanvas.co.uk
Kirghiz-style yurts, groundsheets and custom covers for self-built yurt frames.

Atelier des Trois Yourtes
33 0 299 078478
www.yourtes.fr
A French builder of Kirghiz-style yurts.

FAM
Korycany 12
277 45 Uzice, Czech Republic
420 777 769 145 • 420 315 693 058
Fax: 420 315 693 906
www.fam.ca
info@famtents.com
Manufacturer and distributor of Mongolian-
style yurts and FAM tents. Distributors in France,
Great Britian, Holland, Denmark and Italy.

Fairlove Yurts
Venton House
Dartington, Devon, TQ9 6DP, United Kingdom
www.tfairloveyurts.co.uk
mail@tfairloveyurts.co.uk
Coppiced-wood Turkic-style yurts for sale and rent.

Groovy Yurts
Yves Ballenegger
5247 Lasalle Blvd.
Montreal, QC, H4H 1P
1 888.groovyy
www.groovyyurts.com
info@groovyyurts.com
Importing Mongolian yurts modified for
the North american climate.

Hearthworks, LTD
Mr. Tara Weightman
Spring Cottage
Wormister, North Wootton Shepton Mallet, Somerset BA44AJ
44 0 1749 899521
www.hearthworks.co.uk
info@hearthworks.co.uk
Experience the goodness in simple living, close to the earth.
We manufacture and rent the nest quality yurts and tipis.

<u>Highland Yurts</u>
Paul Spencer
Aberdeenshire, Scotland
01975651734 • 07814051388
www.highlandyurts.com
yurtman0@gmail.com
We are based in the remote Highlands of Scotland sourcing
the exact trees needed to make our various types of yurts.
Whether traditional nomadic living or creating sacred space
in the back garden, our yurts are made with love and care. We
use the most environmentally low impact methods available
so our yurts are made with character and individual charm.

Jurte.info
Bonn, Germany
49 0 228 6299662 • 41 0 32 511 9612
www.jurte.info
info@mongoleishop.de
Importing Mongolian yurts since 2000 for the European market.

Liber Tente
Aureille, France
33 0 623 14 40 65 • 33 0 6 24 97 88 83
www.vivrelayourte.fr
vivrelayourte@free.fr
A French couple builds traditionally-based yurts and tipis.

Little Foot Yurts
Selene and Alex Cole
RR#1 1459 White Rock Road
Wolfville, Nova Scotia B4P 2R1
902.670.4556
www.lfy.ca
info@lfy.ca
Canadian couple makes a unique version of the
traditional yurt and leads yurt-making workshops.

Mongolian Artisan's Aid Foundation (MAAF)
Mr. Cristo C. Gavilla Gomez & Mrs.
Munkhtuya Lundeg, Directors
Ulaanbaatar 15160
C.P.O.Box 2567
Mongolia
976 11 311051
Fax: 976 11 327503
www.samarmagictours.com
sales@samarmagictours.com
Imports gers made by Mongolian artisans,
traditional furnishings and stoves.

The Authentic Mongolian Yurt Company
Monmouthshire, United Kingdom
077885 246641
www.mongolianyurts.co.uk
peter@mongolianyurts.co.uk
Importing Mongolian yurts with 100% felt
and canvas coverings for the UK.

The Mongolian Yurt
Planegger Str 135
81241 München, Germany
40 0 89 139385 95
www.mongolyurt.com
schorsch@jurte.com
Importing Mongolian gers for the German
market. The original mobile home!

Nooitmeerhaast
The Netherlands
0031 0 653 929 777
www.nooitmeerhaast.nl
info@nooitmeerhaast.nl
Dutch and Mongolian manufacturers of authentic Mongolian
gers. Euroyurts fabrication workshop in Ulaan Bataar, Mongolia.
Master builder Froit is the author of *The Real Mongol Ger*.

NYC Mongol
Kallisti Publishing Inc.
Attn: Luigi Kapaj
PO Box 80404
Staten Island, NY 10308
718.984.8736
nycmongol.com
mongol@NYCMongol.com
Importers of Mongolian gers and cultural
items for the SCA community.

Roundhouse Yurts
Tina Hyde
The Forge Cottage
Michaelchurch Escley
Herefordshire, HR2 0JW
07825 432895
www.theroundhouse.uk.com
info@theroundhouse.uk.com
Handcrafted Turkic-style yurts.

Spirits Intent
6 Thornes Park,
Monckton Road,
Wakefield, WF2 7AN, UK
07825 432895
www.spiritsintent.com
spiritintent@yahoo.co.uk
Nomadic European yurt makers with a focus on campgrounds
and commercial accounts. Specializing in yurt covers and palace
yurts, also offering an online yurt cover-making course.

Tio Pancho's Yurts
Sam and Alice
Taos, New Mexico
505.577.4852
www.tiopanchosyurts.blogspot.com
tiopanchosyurts@gmail.com
Building artistic yurts with custom designs for travel and mobility.

Turkoman Gers
Hal Wynne-Jones
Twizzlestone Piece, Lime Kiln Lane
Bisley, Stroud
Gloucestershire, UK GL6 7AS
44 1452 771212
Rental gers for special occasions and Turkic-style gers for sale.

Vishai
Los Angeles, California
323.463.1107 • 323.270.2215 • 323.841.2021
www.vishai.com
info@vishai.com
Importer of yurts from Mongolia with a
foundation to benefit Mongolia's nomads.

Woodland Yurts
Unit 2 Burnt House Farm
Chelvey Road, Backwell, BS48 4AD United Kingdom
01275 879705 • 07969 451009 (workshop)
www.woodlandyurts.co.uk
yurts@woodlandyurts.co.uk
Mongolian and Turkic-style yurts since 1991.

Workshop Under the Hill
Alexandr Sprado
Povltavska 41
250 67 Klecany, Czech Republic
420 723 257915
www.yourtent.com
workshop@yourtent.com
Traditional yurts. Website in Czech, German and
English with forums and extensive photo gallery.

World Tents
David Field
Redfield
Buckingham Road
Winslow, Buckinghamshire, MK18 3LZ
1296 714555
www.worldtents.co.uk
info@worldtents.co.uk
Yurts plus tipi tents, marquee tents,
historical tents and canvas cabins.

The Yurt Workshop
Robert Matthews
21 Calle Baja
Cadiar, Granada, 18448 Spain
44 20 8123 6241 • 34 958 768 806
www.yurtworkshop.com
rob@yurtworkshop.com
Mongolian, Turkey & Iranian yurts. Extensive website.

Yurtastic
Richard Lee
1518 Somona Blvd, Vallejo, California 94590
415.621.2738
www.yurtasticyurts.com
zensella@earthlink.net
Offering a modern twist on the Traditional yurt

Yurt Specialists
Risinghurst, Oxford, United Kingdom, OX3 8HH
Eliot O'Connor: 7787 567179
eliot.oconnor@yahoo.com
Jessie Liang: 7968 898945
jessielianguk@yahoo.co.uk
yurtspecialists.com
Importers of Mongolian yurts.

Yurtopia
Matt
United Kingdom
7799 630027
www.yurtopia.com
matt@yurtopia.com

Yurtworks
Greyhayes, St. Breward, Bodmin, Cornwall, PL30 4LP
01208 85067
www.yurtworks.co.uk
info@yurtworks.co.uk
Handcrafted Turkic-style yurts.

Yurts For Life
Unit 2, Barkingdon Business Park, Staverton
Totnes, Devon TQ9 6AN
1.   01803 762370 • 07957 578 038
www.yurtsforlife.com
sales@yurtsforlife.com
Talented team makes the most stunning
yurts from locally-sourced Ash.

Zeltwelt
Grossholzstrasse 6
Postfach 158
8253 Diessenhofen, Switzerland
41 0 52 657 58 58
www.zeltwelt.ch
info@zeltwelt.ch
In addition to yurts, we offer tipis, chapiteau,
knight tents and outdoor tents.

Tapered Wall Yurts

JADE Craftsman Builders
Dan Neumeyer
Whidbey Island, Washington
360.331.2964
www.jadecraftsmanbuilders.com
dneumeryer@aol.com
Dan integrates yurts based on Bill Coperthwaite's
designs into standard building designs.

Medicine Circle Eco-Retreat
David Kirchhof
P. O. Box 1479
Priest River, Idaho 83856
208.448.1305
www.themedicinecircle.org
medicinecircle@gmail.com
Six yurt styles including Mongolian, Tapered Wall, Fabric
and Frame Panel, are made from recycled materials. Regional
services include overnight stay or day tour of yurts, building
of frame panel yurts, building of deck/platforms and set-up
of fabric yurts, as well as yurt-building workshops.

Red Kite Yurts
Perthshire, Scotland.
44 0 1786 826 921
www.redkiteyurts.com
Kyrgyz-style yurts for sale and rent.

The Yurt Foundation
Bill Coperthwaite
Dickinsons Reach
Machaisport, ME 04655
www.yurtfoundation.org/yurtfoundation.php
Established in 1971, The Yurt Foundation works with groups to build yurts as a part of a community or educational experience. The Foundation also sells yurt plans.

Frame Panel Yurts

California Yurts
David Raitt
2101 Wellmar
Ukiah CA 95481
888.CAL.YURT
www.yurtpeople.com
cayurt@yahoo.com
Original designer of modern engineered frame panel yurts.

Goulburn Yurtworks
Mike Shepherd
New South Wales, Australia
2 4821 5931
www.yurtworks.com.au
hello@yurtworks.com.au
Established in 1984, Goulburn Yurtworks offers Frame Panel yurts delivered as kits or erected for the client. Uses include homes, educational facilities, granny flats, B&B's, visitor centers, medical facilities and many other wonderful uses.

Mandala Custom Homes

Box 234, Nelson, British Columbia, V1L 5P9

866.352.5503

www.mandalahomes.com

info@mandalahomes.com

Canada's round home builder, emphasizing responsibly harvested wood and nontoxic materials.

Medicine Circle Eco-Retreat

David Kirchhof

P. O. Box 1479

Priest River, Idaho 83856

208.448.1305

www.themedicinecircle.org

medicinecircle@gmail.com

Six yurt styles including Mongolian, Tapered Wall, Fabric and Frame Panel, are made from recycled materials. Regional services include overnight stay or day tour of yurts, building of frame panel yurts, building of deck/platforms and set-up of fabric yurts, as well as yurt-building workshops.

Smiling Woods Yurts

Chris Doree

P.O. Box 151

Carlton, Washington 98814

509.560.4424

www.smilingwoodsyurts.com

chris@smilingwoodsyurts.com

A cooperatively owned business working to build community through right livelihood, environmental consciousness, integrity and a joyful, healthy work space. We build solid wall wooden yurt kits with metal roofs, real windows and thermal skylights. Complete yurt kits and roof kits are available in five sizes ranging from 20'-41' diameters. We ship international.

Solargon
1901 E. Prospect Rd.
Fort Collins, Colorado 80525
970.282.7477
www. solargon.com
info@solargon.com

Solargons are octagonal buildings featuring passive solar design principles. The shape is inspired by design elements from Native American and Asian nomadic tribes, while the materials represent the latest in green building technologies. We have created structures that work with and within the environment for outstanding performance, comfort and functionality.

Yurtz by Design
20673 Langley Bypass
Langley BC V3A 5E8
604.576.9878 • 855.576.9878
www.yurtzbydesign.com
info@yurtzbydesign.com

Canada's number one yurt manufacturer.

Camping Yurts, Etc.

Bender's Bjurts
www.bjurtyurt.com
bender@bjurtyurt.com

A Bjurt is a portable structure inspired by Ghengis Khan. Like a yurt, the Bjurt is stable, roomy, and with a vaulted ceiling allows heat to rise. It is sturdy and withstands high desert winds. The Bjurt is a design which concentrates on the primary mechanism of the yurt, the expandable latticework wall, and distills and harnesses it as the fundamental element of a structure that transforms from a bundle of poles into a self-reinforced dome-like frame. It is fast to set up and small to store.

Camping Yurts
541.943.3268 office • 541.410.1630
P.O. Box 1, Summer Lake
Oregon 97640
campingyurts.com
richard@campingyurts.com
Camping yurts are lightweight, portable shelters, ideal for family camping, vacations, temporary accommodation, special events, or even weddings. They are very spacious with lots of head room, yet pack down small and can be easily loaded on a car roof. The industry's leading makers of ultra-light yurts for those on the go. We also offer custom yurt homes designed for the future and built to last

Clean Air Yurts
30 Crispall Lane
New Palz, New York 12561
845.633.2875
www.cldeanairyurts.com
matt@cleanaireyurts.com
The industry's leading maker of ultra-light yurts for those on the go. We also offer yurt homes designed for the future and built to last.

GoYurt Shelters
Portland, Oregon
877.446.9878
www.gourt.com
info@goyurt.com
Truly portable yurts, 13' diameter, designed to be lightweight yet rugged. Innovative features allow for fast set-up and easy transport.

Mountain Wind Yurts
Dave Cruey
Cypress, Texas 77429
281.807.3440 or 281.627.3621
www.mountainwindyurts.com
dave@mountainwindyurts.com

Two different sizes of yurts are available—12' and 16'. Every yurt we make comes complete with all you need from start to finish, with the exception of a level area and the cement blocks to set the yurt up on. Our yurt's structure is 100% metal to make them strong, long lasting and easy to setup. They consist of two floor pans, two wall sections, 16 rafters and a compression ring. They can be built by two to three people in four to five hours depending on skill levels.

Rainier Yurts
18375 Olympic Ave.
South Seattle, Washington 98188
800.869.7162 • 425.981.1203
www.rainieryurts.com
sales@rainieryurts.com

The "Sparrow", a 12' OR 14' diameter yurt designed for easy assembly with an optional vinyl floor for camping.

Traders of Tamerlane
Ewing, New Jersey
609.433.3248
www.tradersoftamerlane.com
contact@tradersoftamerlane.com

Affordable handmade yurts for camping in comfort; yurt rentals and accessories.

Yurta
Larkland Highlands, Quebec
877.807.5008 • 905.831.0418
www.yurta.ca
info@yurta.ca
Yurt-inspired 17' structure designed for portablilty and easy set-up.

Yurtastic
Richard Lee
1518 Somona Blvd, Vallejo, California 94590
415.621.2738
www.yurtasticyurts.com
zensella@earthlink.net
Offering a modern twist on the Traditional yurt

Yurts Of America
4375 Sellers Street
Indianapolis, Indianapolis
317.377.9879
www.yurtsofamerica
info@yurtsofamerica.com
Safe and reliable camp structures for kids and/or families.

Vacation in a Yurt

In Hawaii:
Chic Eco Yurt Home & Edible Gardens
Pahoa, Hawaii
www.airbnb.com/rooms/128886

Hangin' Loose on the Big Island
Keaau, Hawaiian
www.airbnb.com/rooms/28739

Adventures Lava Rock Hale
www.airbnb.com/rooms/1530219

Worldwide:
Cedar House Inn & Yurts
Mary Beth and Fred Tanner, Hosts
6463 Highway 19 North
Dahlonega, GA 30533
706.867.9446
www.georgiamountaininn.com
info@georgiamountaininn.com
Enjoy one of our two unique yurts tucked into the
woods behind the inn. Breakfast is included.

El Capitan Canyon
11560 Calle Real
Santa Barbara, California 93117
866.352.2729
www.elcapitancanyon.com
info@elcapitancanyon.com
Six "Adventure Yurts" each provide accommodations for a
family of four, electricity, bathhouse, picnic tables and fire pit.

Falling Waters Resort
10345 US Hwy. 74 West
Bryson City, North Carolina 28713
800.451.9972
Fax: 864.647.5361
www.fallingwatersresort.com
wwltd@nuvox.net
Located in the middle of one of the premier outdoor activity
areas in the world, and adjacent to the Nantahala Gorge, with
outstanding whitewater rafting, zipline canopy tours, mountain
biking, horseback riding, fishing, canoeing and kayaking.

Hinsdale Haute Route

P. O. Box 771
Lake City, Colorado 81235
970.944.2269
www.hinsdalehauteroute.com
grayj@lakecity.net

The highest hut system in Colorado. Currently offering two yurts on a year round basis:

The Jon Wilson Memorial Yurt is one and a quarter miles from the trailhead at Highway 149. It is a great destination for families with youngsters or beginning to novice backcountry hut users. It also makes a good start for a trip to the Colorado Trail Friends Yurt. It's close proximity to the trailhead allows groups to drive for hours, arriving at the trailhead in mid-afternoon and still have time to reach the yurt before sunset.

The Colorado Trail Friends Yurt provides a welcome, warm and dry respite for many Colorado Trail and Continental Divide Trail hikers in summer. In winter, groups using the Colorado Trail Friends Yurt should be of strong intermediate to expert capabilities.

www.hipcamp.com

Discover unique experiences in renting on private ranches, nature preserves, farms, vineyards, and public campgrounds across the U.S. Book yurts, tent camping, tree houses, cabins, primitive backcountry sites, car camping, airstreams, tiny houses, RV camping, glamping tents and more.

Maine Forest Yurts
David Crowley Family
430 Auburn-Pownal Road
Durham, Maine 04222
(207) 400-5956
www.maineforestyurts.com
yurts@mainforestyurts.com
Our campground is located on Runaround Pond in
Durham, Maine and spans over 100 acres of wilderness.
Our fully furnished yurts are a perfect way to experience
glamping! We re conveniently located near Bradbury
Mountain State Park, Freeport/L.L. Bean and Portland.

Ravenhouse Alaska Bed & Breakfast
Andrew Pruitt
72271 Valley Side Ave.
Anchor Point, Alaska 99556907.299.5473
www.ravenhousealaska.com
(Also on VRBO)
What used to be the center of an old Homestead from
1951 has now been renovated and turned into a Bed
And Breakfast, located three miles from Anchor River,
and two miles north of Anchor Point Town Center.

Roundhouse Yurts
Tina Hyde
The Forge Cottage
Michaelchurch Escley
Herefordshire, HR2 0JW
07825 432895
www.theroundhouse.uk.com
info@theroundhouse.uk.com
Sleep in our cosy and magical yurts. Yurt hire for
slumber parties, children, adults, camping, even
romantic wedding night yurts. Just heavenly.

sykescottages.co.uk
Yurt rentals in the United Kingdom.

The Yurt Workshop
Robert Matthews
21 Calle Baja
Cadiar, Granada, 18448 Spain
44 20 8123 6241 • 34 958 768 806
www.yurtworkshop.com/yurts/yurtrentals.aspx

State Parks
Many parks and forests within a specific state park
system offer yurt rental accommodations. Please check
each park website. In addition, www.reserveamerica.com
handles reservations for this unique rental option.

Arizona State Parks
928.337.4441
www.azstateparks.com

Arkansas State Parks
800.737.8355
www.degray.com

B.C. Provincial Parks
www.env.gov.bc.ca/bcparks/recreation/yurts

Colorado State Parks
www.parks.state.co.us/reservations/yurtinformation

Georgia State Parks Cloudland Canyon State Park
770.784.3152
www.gastateparks.org

Florida State Parks
850.643.2674
www.floridastateparks.org/torreya/default.cfm

Idaho State Parks
888.9campid • 888.922.6743
www.parksandrecreation.idaho.gov

Kansas State Parks
www.ksoutdoors.com/Eisenhower-State-Park
www.kdwp.state.ks.us

Manitoba Provincial Parks
888.482.2267
In Winnipeg, call 948.3333
www.gov.mg.ca

Maryland State Parks
301.387.5563
www.dnr.state.md.us

Massachusetts State Parks
978.939.8962
www.mass.gov

Michigan State Parks
800.447.2757
www.michigandnr.com

Missouri State Parks
800.334.6946
www.mostateparks.com

Montana State Parks
406.751.4577
www.fwp.mt.gov

Nevada State Parks
775.289.1693
wardcharcoalovens@sbcglobal.net
www.parks.nv.gov

New Hampshire State Parks
603.271.3556
www.nhstateparks.org
nhparks@dred.state.nh.us

New Jersey State Parks
www.state.nj.us

North Dakota State Parks
800.807.4723
www.parkrec.nd.gov

Ohio State Parks
www.ohiodnr.com

Ontario Parks
www.OntarioParks.com

Oregon State Parks
800.452.5687
www.oregon.gov

Pennsylvania State Parks
888.PA.PARKS
www.pa.reserveworld.com

Quebec Provincial Parks
418.337.2900
In Quebec – 800.321.4992
www.bonjourquebec.com

Rhode Island State Parks
401.322.7337
www.riparks.com

Virginia State Parks
757.331.2267
www.dcr.virginia.gov

Washington State Parks
www.parks.wa.gov

General Websites for Yurt Rentals
www.travelchannel.com/interests/luxury/articles/lusury-yurts
Modern luxury yurt resorts around the world.

www.more.com/lifestyles/travel/
who-needs-tent-9-best-yurts-retreats-us
The nine best yurt retreats in the United States.

www.yurts.com/yurt-vacations
Vacation in a Pacific Yurt.

www.curbed.com/2016/7/22/12252416/
camping-yurts-vacation-for-rent
Five vacation yurts to get away from it all:
Snow Mountain Ranch in Winter Park, Colorado
Garden Yurt in Ithaca, New York
Jimmy Keen Yurt in Moab, Utah
Shearwater Cove in Seward, Alaska
Shenandoah Crossing Resort in Virginia

www.glampinghub.com/rentalsearch/yurts

www.yurtlodging.com
Yurt rentals in Alaska, Arkansas, California, Colorado, Georgia,
Hawaii, Idaho, Indiana, Maine, Michigan, Minnesota, Montana,
New Hampshire, New York, North Carolina, Oklahoma, Oregon,
Utah, Virginia, Washington, Wisconsin and Wyoming.

WORKSHOPS

Little Foot Yurts
www.lfy.ca
info@lfy.ca

Nooitmeerhaast
www.nooitmeerhaast.com

Red Kite Yurts
www.redkiteyurts.com

Spirits Intent
6 Thornes Park,
Monckton Road,
Wakefield, WF2 7AN, UK
07825 432895
www.spiritsintent.com
spiritsintent@yahoo.co.uk
Online yurt cover-making course.

The Yurt Foundation
www.yurtfoundation.org/yurtfoundation.php

GENERAL INFORMATION

One Island Sustainable Living
www.oneisland.org

One Island is a non-profit sustainability program serving rural coastal areas of Hawaii, California and Washington. In response to the challenges of our time, our programs foster connections between inspired teachers, designers and learners to strengthen creativity and resiliency in remote rural communities. Programs focus on short, easy-to-implement projects and longer term strategic sustainability efforts.

Goulburn Yurtworks
Mike Shepherd
New South Wales, Australia
2 4821 5931
www.yurtworks.com.au
hello@yurtworks.com.au
Offers a yurtfarm camp to teach farm and bush skills to children.

Love Yurts
44 0 7899846330 • 44 0 7980841886
www.loveyurts.com
info@loveyurts.com
In addition to fabric yurt sales, we offer expert advice on eco-services such as solar, heating and sanitation solutions for your yurts and hire services for major festivals, events, weddings, corporate functions and retreats.

North American Yurt Alliance (NAYA)

www.yurtalliance.com

NAYA is an international alliance of yurt companies from across North America working together to maintain industry standards while addressing common issues like building code compliance, insurance, and the development of ecological materials.

simplydifferently.org

Information on building yurts, as well as tipis and domes. Includes calculations.

Stephan's Florilegium

www. florilegium.org, under "Structures" and then "Yurts" Interview with Bill Coperthwaite: www.herondance. org/Bill_Coperthwaite_W9.cfm

www.mongolyurt.com

An excellent resource for information pertaining to the history and construction of Mongolian yurts. Also includes a photo library.

Yurt Forum

www.yurtforum.com

Join the Yurt Community, jumping in on lively discussions about yurts and yurt living! Extensive information on purchasing, building, and living in a yurt. Be sure to check out our Book Store!

yurtinfo.org

A comprehensive educational website originally established by Becky Kemery, author of *Yurts: Living in The Round*, providing both information and inspiration while assisting the worldwide yurt community in making valuable connections.

SUPPLIERS

Albion Canvas Company
Unit 6, Barkingdon Business Park Staverton, Totnes
Devon, UK TQ9 6AN
0845.456.9290 (local rate)
44 0 1803 762230
www.albioncanvas.co.uk
Groundsheets and custom covers for self-built yurt frames.

Atelier des Trois Yourtes
33 0 299 078478
www.yourtes.fr
Furnishings and accessories.

Blue Spruce Enterprise
613.824.0839
www.blue-spruce.ca
yurts@blue-spruce.ca
Supplies alternative energy systems. Located in Ontario, Canada.

Colorado Yurt Company
P.O. Box 1626
28 W. South 4th Street
Montrose, Colorado 81401
800.288.3190 • 970.240.2111
www.coloradoyurt.com
ivy@coloradoyurt.com
Fabric wall and roof covers for 16' to 30' yurts using heavy-duty,
industrial fabrics. Domes and compression rings are also available.

Craftwood Yurt Installations & Interior Designs, LLC
www.facebook.com/Craftwoodyurts
Craftwood is a family owned and operated yurt installation business. We are the sole commercial installer for Nomad Shelter yurts out of Homer, Alaska.

NYC Mongol
Kallisti Publishing Inc.
Attn: Luigi Kapaj
PO Box 80404
Staten Island, NY 10308
718.984.8736
www.nycmongol.com
mongol@nycmongol.com
Importers of cultural items for the SCA community.

Round Foot Homes
P.O. Box 17
Fort Collins, Colorado 80522
970.472.2394
www.roundfoothomes.com
info@roundroothomes.com
We provide detailed plans giving all the information you need to construct your own Green Home." We can help you choose a manufacturer or dealer, and we offer continued support throughout the building process.

Sagebrush Tipi Works
Debra
Davenport, Washington
509.690.7303
www.sagebrushtipiworks.com
info@sagebrushtipiworks.com
Custom-fit replacement covers for fabric yurts
using 12oz marine Sunforger fabric.

Spirits Intent
6 Thornes Park,
Monckton Road,
Wakefield, WF2 7AN, UK
07825 432895
www.spiritsintent.com
spiritsintent@yahoo.co.uk
Yurt covers.

Traders of Tamerlane
Ewing, New Jersey
609.433.3248
www.tradersoftamerlane.com
contact@tradersoftamerlane.com
Decor, furniture and other goods from cultures across Asia, both
past and present. All of our products are individually made with
care and our craftsmen take pride in every piece they produce.

Woodland Yurts
Unit 2 Burnt House Farm
Chelvey Road, Backwell, BS48 4AD United Kingdom
01275 879705 • 07969 451009 (workshop)
www.woodlandyurts.co.uk
yurts@woodlandyurts.co.uk
Mongolian and Turkic-style yurt plans.

BOOKS

Yurts: Living in the Round
Kemery, Becky. Gibbs Smith, 2006 the definitive source
of information, both past and present, concerning
the world of yurts. Full color photographs.

A HANDMADE LIFE: In Search of Simplicity
Coperthwaite, Wm. S.: Chelsea Green Publishing Company, 2003
Richly illustrated with luminous color photographs
by Peter Forbes, A Handmade
Life is a moving and inspirational testament
to a new practice of old ways of life.

The Complete Yurt Handbook
King, Paul. Batn: Eco-Logic Books, 2001
Includes instructions on how to make both Mongolian and
Turkic yurts. Emphasis is on traditional Central Asian yurts.

Home Work: Handbuilt Shelter
Kahn, Lloyd. Bolinas, CA: Shelter Publications 2004
Offers a section on Bill Coperthwaite's yurts,
as well as information on Mongolian gers.

Mongolian Cloud Houses: How to Make
a Yurt and Live Comfortably
Kuehn, Dan Frank, Bolinas, CA:
Shelter Publications 2006
Drawings and step-by-step instructions for building
a low-cost yurt with a bamboo framework.

The Big Adventures Of Tiny House
www.thebigadventuresoftinyhouse.com
A delightful children's story of adventure and community,
and most importantly a fresh take on the meaning of home.
"With a tug and a thump and a boppity-bump...away we go!"

BLOGS
www.livingintheround.org
www.tinyhouseblog.com
www.yurtworkshop.com
www.shelterdesigns.net
www.greenhs.com.au

TV, Cable and Satellite Programs

HGTV
www.hgtv.com/shows/shows-a-z
Tiny House Arrest
Tiny House Builders
Tiny House Hunters
Tiny House Jamboree
Tiny House, Big Living
Tiny Luxury

DIY Network
www.diynetwork.com/shows/shows-a-z
Love Yurts
Tiny House Jamboree
Tiny House, Big Living
Tiny Luxury

Events
National Tiny House Jamboree
www.tinyhousejamboree.com

Jen is available...

...as a speaker for your upcoming women's
conferences, retreats and meetings.

For booking information:
jenmcgeehan1@gmail.com
808.747.2365

About the Author

Jen McGeehan is a motivational speaker, sharing her humorous yet inspiring stories of God's miraculous healing and restoration. As an accomplished equestrian and nature enthusiast, Jen was able to successfully transition from life in the fast lane of Southern California to the off-grid, back-to-nature farm life of the Hamakua Coast of Hawaii. She is the founder of the Annual Christian Women's Gathering, currently held on the Big Island of Hawaii. And she is a voice within the Tiny House Movement, both in Hawaii and beyond!

CPSIA information can be obtained
at www.ICGtesting.com
Printed in the USA
FSHW022030081019
62824FS